The Little
Ed Book

D1600624

WHEN THE BELL RINGS

The Little Ed Book

Guy Claxton

University of London
Institute of Education

Routledge & Kegan Paul
London, Henley and Boston

0379860

First published in 1978
by Routledge & Kegan Paul Ltd
39 Store Street,
London WC1E 7DD.
Broadway House,
Newtown Road,
Henley-on-Thames,
Oxon RG9 1EN and
9 Park Street,
Boston, Mass. 02108, USA
Set in 10 on 11 pt IBM Journal Roman
by Hope Services, Wantage, Oxon.
and printed in Great Britain by
Lowe & Brydone Ltd, Thetford
© Guy Claxton, 1978
No part of this book may be reproduced in
any form without permission from the
publisher, except for the quotation of brief
passages in criticism

British Library Cataloguing in Publication Data

Claxton, Guy

   The little ed book.
   1. Education
   I. Title
   370'.2'4372   LB17   77-30691

   ISBN 0 7100 8868 X

Contents

0379860

To my mother and father

Acknowledgments

The author and publishers are grateful for permission to quote from the following works:

The Collected Poems of Louis MacNeice, and *Collected Poems* by Stephen Spender; reprinted by permission of Faber & Faber.

The Glass Bead Game by Herman Hesse; reprinted by permission of the Estate of Herman Hesse, R. and C. Winston and Jonathan Cape.

Cat's Cradle by Kurt Vonnegut Jr; reprinted by permission of John Farquharson.

'Education on the Non-Verbal Level' by Aldous Huxley; reprinted by permission of *Daedalus*, Journal of the American Academy of Arts and Sciences, Boston, Massachusetts, Spring 1962, *Science and Technology in Contemporary Society*.

Zen Buddhism and Psychoanalysis by E. Fromm, D. Suzuki and R. de Martino; reprinted by permission of Souvenir Press.

The School that I'd Like by E. Blishen; reprinted by permission of Penguin Books Ltd.

Frank brought Mona to her father's cave and left us alone.

We had difficulty in speaking at first. I was shy.

Her gown was diaphanous. Her gown was azure. It was a simple gown, caught lightly at the waist by a gossamer thread. All else were shaped by Mona herself. Her breasts were like pomegranates or what you will, but like nothing so much as a young woman's breasts.

Her feet were all but bare. Her toenails were exquisitely manicured. Her scanty sandals were gold.

'How — how do you do?' I asked. My heart was pounding. Blood boiled in my ears.

'It is not possible to make a mistake,' she assured me.

I did not know that this was a customary greeting given by all Bokononists when meeting a shy person.

KURT VONNEGUT Jr (*Cat's Cradle*)

If you want to make sense, I've learned, you should never use the word *should* or *ought* until after you've used the word *if*.

JOHN BARTH (*The Floating Opera*)

Introduction

It is my conviction that to withstand and counteract
the deadening impact of mass society, a man's work
must be permeated by his personality. Just as his choice
of work must not be due to mere convenience, chance
or expediency, but should directly reflect how he
reaches for self-realization in this world of ours, so the
results of his work, besides being objectively purposeful,
should also reflect his own purposes in life.

Bruno Bettelheim

This book is for people who are becoming, or have recently
become, teachers, and for any others interested in teaching.

It contains a collection of thoughts, questions, suggestions and information about education. They relate more to
personal and practical issues than theoretical ones; they are,
to be accurate, about *you* in education, rather than about
education itself.

Any comments I make are emphatically *not* prescrip-
tions for success: they are ideas to be tried on for size. Only
if you find that they fit will they be of any use.

I have tried to write as neutrally as possible; to be questioning but not doctrinaire. Of course I have failed. The
fact that there are some issues I consider to be worth thinking about, and others not, is a value judgment. However I
have tried not to push my answers (in so far as I have any).

The fundamental belief that guides me is the importance
of interpersonal issues in education, that who 'you' are
determines what kind of a teacher 'you' will be more than
anything else. Many of my questions will be about 'you'.

Another belief is that answers to important questions
are neither quick, easy nor 'right'. Don't expect that you
will be able to solve these things overnight, or that other
people will be able to solve them for you. On the other

hand, many of these issues oughtn't to be ignored: it's a big responsibility being a teacher, and learning to be one is a serious business.

In fact, writing and revising this have turned out to be significant stages in my own developing thinking about education. I wrote the first edition in October 1975 and am revising it now at the beginning of November 1976; it is very interesting to look back and see how much my attitudes and preoccupations have changed in the course of a year. In some ways I seem now to believe more strongly than ever in the need for every individual to work out and be responsible for his own actions and opinions, and in the need for this to be fostered in young people by the presence of genuine trust and care in their relationships with their teachers. And yet at the same time my sympathy and respect for the traditional type of benevolently authoritarian teacher has increased enormously. Both Herbert Kohl and the master (whose name I forget for the moment) in Rattigan's *The Browning Version* seem admirable to me.

It is awkward being stuck with apparently conflicting views like this; other people tend to resent what they see as the inconsistency it breeds. I remember one of my students expressing great anger and disappointment with me in a seminar for daring to take Skinner and his reward-and-punishment teaching technology seriously; he had only seen my 'humanistic' side before, and now I was letting him down.

Yet I do not feel inconsistent in myself, nor do I think that my 'eclecticism' is born of indifference. It is not that I feel committed to neither side; I feel committed to both. And I suspect that the resolution lies in a deeper sense of what 'trust', 'sympathy', 'kindness', etc. mean, than I had before. The compassion of a Zen master, or a parent, sometimes shows itself in a blow, and a real concern for his students may make a teacher stern. What *matters*, I am coming to believe, is the spirit in which actions are done, and which communicates itself in the unanalysable and unintentional aura in which all our actions are wrapped.

Thus, while this time last year the 'aura' of my writing was saying 'progressive is best', even while the words themselves expressed indifference, this year my trust in a wide variety of styles is more genuine, and my belief in the importance of the actor over that of the costume is concomitantly higher. Almost certainly this has led to inconsistencies of tone, if not of content, in the text, for I have not re-written it all, by any means.

A more general shift in my own learning I find more difficult to cope with in this book. October 1975 found me exploring, trying on for size, and taking in ideas deriving from psychotherapy and the psychology of personal growth and self-actualization; and while it is not obvious to all, these ideas do have direct implications for institutional education, many of which have been spelt out by the originators of the ideas themselves — chiefly Carl Rogers and Abraham Maslow. A typical event from this time was my reading *One Flew Over the Cuckoo's Nest*, and writing 'This applies to school!' rather savagely in the margin. Now I have moved on from there, in ways which have felt quite natural and logical, to an approach to education exemplified by Aldous Huxley's *Island*, and which is leading me to investigate the comparative theologies and philosophies of East and West. Keynote books now would be Fromm, Suzuki and de Martino's *Zen and Psychoanalysis*, Alan Watts's *The Book on the Taboo Against Knowing Who You Are* and Paul Tillich's *The Courage to Be*. Yet it would require a different book to explain why on earth the Abbot of Engakuji temple in Kamakura has anything to say to Jude Hemming in Woodberry Down School — or indeed to Guy Claxton at the Institute of Education. So I have had to content myself with just a few favourite quotes, and concentrate again on things less esoteric.

The style of the book is intended to be personal, tentative and fairly snappy — partly because this way of writing comes quite naturally, and also because I enjoy reading books by other people written in this way. I have tried to write in snippets, which may act as seed-crystals to precipitate the crystallization of your own thought, either by sympathy with or reaction against. From the feedback I have had to the home-produced first edition, this aim seems to have been met for many people, but not for all. For one critic in particular the tone has come over not as 'tentative and succinct', but as 'uncertain and condescending'. In revising, I have tried to be aware of this and correct it, where I agree.

The book is organized into five sections. The first introduces some general questions about people in education — issues that the person-behind-the-professional must answer for himself. The second is a kind of dictionary, with a more practical flavour, of situations and ideas which are forever cropping up, and of some ways of responding to them that you might want to try out. Both of these sections are larded with quotations whose only unifying characteristic is that they have all provoked, outraged or 'amused' me into thinking more clearly about where I stand. The third is an essay, written two years ago by a student of mine, Anna Wilkinson, about her personal reactions to her early days as a teacher, which captures most vividly the immediacy of some of the things that Parts 1 and 2 have mentioned. The fourth is a small section on the teacher and the law — a topic which strikes me as important and which, as far as I know, our students here at the Institute don't actually get told anything about. The fifth is an annotated reading list of my 'formative' books, which includes philosophy, theology, psychotherapy, mysticism and fiction.

Finally, if I were to suggest how to use this book, I'd say 'read it through, then find a few people you think you could learn to trust to discuss your attitudes to Part 1, keep the rest for reference, and try a few of the books'. If it doesn't work as a stimulus to you to work some things out, it won't have worked at all.

To facilitate your arguing with me, the book is laid out fairly spaciously, so that you can write on it. I find it interesting and useful to note my immediate reactions (whether 'Bullshit!' or 'Spot on!'), and easier to do it on the book than separately. If this is a library copy, however, it would be public-spirited to deny yourself this pleasure.

The title, by the way, isn't an exhortation to revolution. It's just a joke.

Guy Claxton

Part 1

Some Basic
Questions

What are my ideals for education?

You may well feel it is important to have an idea about what *you* believe about education, as well as about what other people think. Do you think it's important (a) to induct children into established bodies of knowledge/modes of thinking (and what does this mean?); (b) to provide them with useful facts (how banks work) and skills (car maintenance); (c) to introduce them to the delights of art, literature and music; (d) to train their minds (what does *this* mean?); (e) to socialize them (i.e. teach them accepted ways of behaving and getting on with people); (f) to help them to grow in their abilities to be autonomous, responsible and make decisions; etc.

We might divide rationales for education into three: giving children what they *want*, *need* and *ought* to know. Some people would argue for each of these, but there isn't a single, obvious answer. If your 10-year-old *wanted* to learn about oral sex or torture, would you tell her? If you believed she *ought* to go to Sunday school, but she hated it, would you make her? Do all children *need* to read at 6 years old? (Most people would say 'yes', but if a child *really* needed to know something, wouldn't he want to learn it automatically?)

What are the relative needs of individual and State?

The aims of education may be either individual- or society-directed. Critics of education say it serves the ends of society far too much; the individual gets lost in the demand of society for people who will do what they're told, when they're told, willingly, for material reward. Education, they say, doesn't foster creativity and individual responsibility — it tries to eliminate them. Even if there is some truth in this, should we swing entirely to the opposite extreme? An island full of anarchists would probably be worse even than an island full of automata. It may be that the priorities need shifting back towards the individual, but how far?

The whole question of the relationship between education and the State is very complicated. If you are politically/sociologically inclined this is an issue that may interest and inflame you; on the other hand it may bore you to tears. Is it *necessary* to think about it if it doesn't interest you? Should you have views about everything? If not, do you expect children to have views about things that don't interest *them*? If yes, is it fair? What makes them different?

How hard can I push?

Suppose a child — your child, let's say — didn't want to learn something that you genuinely believed he ought to know. How much persuasion can you allow yourself to use? I imagine a scale of 'force' running from presentation through introduction, suggestion, persuasion and seduction to coercion. How far will your conscience allow you to go before you're prepared to take 'No' for an answer? Do you give a different answer for different things? Would you *make* the child do anything you thought worthwhile/important/a matter of life and death? Would his age matter?

Can I allow him to say 'No'?

Are you capable of allowing people not to be interested in what you're interested in? Suppose you're in the middle of explaining something you care deeply about to someone whose opinion you respect, and he says 'I'm bored', do you feel hurt or put down? (I do.) Most people say you teach better if you're interested in what you're teaching; but it may be more difficult to accept other people's right to be bored. It feels as if it's not just your subject but a bit of *you* that's being turned down.

I may *suggest* to you that you learn X: if you look like declining, I can easily slip into persuading, seducing or even coercing you — not because you need X, but because I can't bear to feel a bit of me being rejected. It's very often difficult to know when this is operating — the needs are buried pretty deep — but you may find it salutary to be aware of the possibility.

Nothing is really explained by its cause or motivation, for we find only causes behind causes until we can pursue them no longer. It is like a child asking 'Why? Why? Why? . . .' until its father, like a Zen master, says 'O shut up and suck your lollipop!'

Alan Watts

Chemists at least can use analysis; patients suffering from a malady whose cause is unknown to them can call in a doctor; criminal cases are more or less cleared up by the examining magistrate. But for the disconcerting actions of our fellow men, we rarely discover the motive.

Marcel Proust

Why do I want to be a teacher?

Questions about motives are always dubious, since they are exercises in rendering actions intelligible to our reason which may have no rational cause. To attribute motives to ourselves is only a slightly less risky business than attributing them to other people. But the attempt may be fruitful if we allow any 'thought' hypotheses that we have to be checked against our intuitive feelings. There is no way of *knowing* whether we acted for this motive or that — but we can tell when a suggestion *feels* right.

Your motives might include:
because I enjoy teaching;
because I feel children ought to know X;
because I couldn't think of anything else to do after university;
God knows, I've *always* wanted to be a teacher;
because my father's a teacher;
because I have a need to be effective in other people's lives;
I like the power;

I like being with children;
I have strong ideas about education that I want to try out;
I'm rapidly coming to the conclusion that I don't, etc.
It's important that you take this question seriously: you may discover that you really *don't* want to teach, or, if you're honest, that being with children makes you anxious and uneasy You may decide, in abstract, that it's better not to be a teacher at all than to teach for the wrong motives — and then find this applying to yourself.

Maybe the fundamental question is not 'Why do I want to teach?' but 'Do I want to teach at all?' It may be rather frightening to take this question seriously — but it's better to find out now than later. There is no dishonour in deciding you don't want to teach. You can't know for sure whether it suits you until you've tried it, and found out a bit about what it is. Not everyone is capable of doing or enjoying everything. That's a fact of life; and if you *don't* want to teach, that's not a *failure* in you, it's a bit of information about you — you're not yet *committed* to becoming a teacher, if you are currently doing a course in teacher training.

Should there be schools?

As you think about what you would like education to be, an idea of your ideal educational system will gradually form in your head. But you may find yourself questioning whether there should be an educational *system*, in the sense of institutions-called-schools-run-by-the-State, at all. You're bound to have heard of the deschoolers — Illich, Goodman, Reimer, Holt — who between them have posed questions about what schools are, and what they are up to, that I for one find difficult to ignore. You may not agree that doing away with schools completely is the answer, in which case you are free to fantasize about how you would like them to be. But if you are inclined to agree that schools should go, that obviously puts you in a sticky position job-wise! It doesn't necessarily mean that you drop out there and then — you may want to finish your training and then work in some kind of 'alternative' set-up. But if there is a conflict between your beliefs (e.g. 'schools must go') and your actions (being on a teacher training course), you can't ignore it.

You may find it interesting and enlightening to crystallize your ideas about schools by actually designing one from scratch. Considering questions like what shape the classrooms would be, would you have compulsory games, or school uniform, how to involve parents, what the timetable would be, etc. makes abstract issues like 'equality', 'responsibility', 'discipline' and 'curriculum' very real. It might also make you more sympathetic to the problems of administration (or you might decide to do away with the administrators altogether and let the children make the decisions!).

What is a teacher?

Pondering on ideals will inevitably raise questions about what exactly the teacher's role should be. There are lots of possible analogies for the role of teacher. Which ones do you accept, and which are incompatible? *Resource*: the teacher as a ministerer to the children's needs. A provider of books, arranger of visits, changer of plugs, etc. *Entertainer*: the teacher as a music hall turn, keeping the children entertained, occupied and perhaps helping them to learn a little bit too. *Friend*: does the role of teacher include being friends with the children? Is it dangerous? Will you lose respect? *Doctor*: the teacher as a diagnoser of various needs of individual children and prescriber of suitable learning treatment. *Cop*: a policeman in the society of school, enforcing the rules of the society, arresting people and sending them for trial. *Judge*: arbitrator of disputes and disher-out of punishments. *Fisherman*: Someone who baits his hook with an appetizing bit of knowledge, and waits patiently for the students to nibble. *Counsellor*: is it part of the teacher's job to deal with the emotional as well as intellectual needs of his pupils? Or does this interfere with his 'teaching' function: should he rather be a *Referral Agency*: distributing children to 'specialists' like the educational psychologist, sanctuary, remedial reading teacher, psychiatrist? *Clerk*: marker of registers, collector of dinner money, orderer of books, guardian of the staffroom coffee fund. How much of a clerk would your ideal teacher be? *Public Relations Officer*: chatting up parents, presenting a suitably rosy picture of a child's progress, and the school's part in it. *Learner*: we don't hear very much

11

about teachers being learners once they've qualified — except when they manage to be seconded on a course. Do *you* think you have anything to learn by being a teacher? Do you think the children have anything to teach you?

> The truth was of course that it is one thing — an easy thing — to give what Cardinal Newman called 'notional' assent to a proposition such as 'There is no justice': quite another and more difficult matter to give it 'real' assent, to learn it stingingly, to the heart, through involvement.
>
> *John Barth*

Can I be my ideal teacher?

Almost certainly not. Herbert Kohl in *The Open Classroom* says 'My beliefs in a free, non-authoritarian classroom always ran ahead of my personal ability to teach in one', and my experience is the same. It's much easier to change one's mental knowledge (attitudes, beliefs, opinions) than one's 'physical' knowledge — the knowledge that controls how we act spontaneously, and how we feel. Kohl goes on, 'A crucial thing to realize is that changing the nature of life in the classroom is no less difficult than changing one's own personality, and every bit as dangerous and time-consuming. It is also as rewarding.' If your ideal classroom matches exactly the one you happen to find yourself in . . . you're very lucky. If not, and if the disparity between ideal and actual troubles you, you're in for a hard time.

A classroom will only work — certainly you will only be happy in it — if you are comfortable with the way you are behaving. It is no use trying to be something you believe in if you can't do it. You will only get frustrated and disillusioned. You may well end up blaming your problems on the children rather than on your own incongruence. You must accept that changing either you or the classroom takes time; it can only happen bit by bit. The function of having an 'ideal you', or an 'ideal classroom', in your mind, it seems to me, ought to be to provide a *direction* to your activities. John Lennon says 'how can I go forward when I don't know which way I'm facing?' Your ideals are landmarks that tell you which way 'forward' is. But if you are impatient, your ideals will simply upset you. I don't have any magic cure for impatience; if you are the sort of person who gets angry when he sees injustice, stupidity and waste, you may decide it's better not to be *too* idealistic.

We know ourselves so little that we can only find out what feels comfortable by experimenting. You will probably find yourself trying out things that you're not sure about. When you do, bear two things in mind. The first is that experiments never fail. They are things we do to *find out* what we can't *work out*; whichever way the result goes is equally valuable. If you find out that you feel uncomfortable acting in a certain way, that's as useful as if you had felt comfortable. We are all unique, we all have our own way of doing things, and we all fall far short of what we would like to be. If one is really capable of accepting that, one will never feel a 'failure'. As Carl Rogers says, 'the facts are friendly'. It's difficult to believe sometimes, but I believe it's true.

The second thing is: experiment gradually. If you find you can't handle a little experiment nothing is lost. But if you bound into your class one morning and say 'I've decided you can do exactly what you want today — no holds barred,' you'll quickly regret it. When chaos ensues, you will almost certainly feel uncomfortable and clamp down again. The children's suspicion that you didn't really mean it will rapidly be confirmed, and they will be less inclined to trust you next time.

There are some things which cannot be learned quickly, and time, which is all we have, must be paid heavily, for their acquiring. They are the very simplest things and because it takes a man's life to know them the little new that each man gets from life is very costly, and the only heritage he has to leave.

Ernest Hemingway

What about pressures from outside?

There are two kinds of things that stop you being your ideal teacher. One is the kind of person you are *now*, which I've talked about already. The other is other people. The demands that are made on you by the school, by the curriculum, by exams, even by the children, may be irreconcilable not only with the ideal you, but with the actual you as well. Very likely you will find yourself having to do things that seem senseless or even vicious, and your self-respect will be in jeopardy. When that happens, people resort to some well-known strategies — they rationalize, they distort the evidence, they deny things, they become dogmatic, they make exceptions. All these reactions effectively prevent you from facing up to the situation, and buy short-term relief at a heavy price in long-term wear-and-tear. If you accept the facts for what they are, you may be able to do something about them — even if it means changing jobs, or leaving teaching altogether. If you don't, not only you but your students will suffer.

What is my ideal person?

Although children are undoubtedly a bit different from adults, and have special needs, what you believe about how you would like yourself and other people to be will obviously influence how you are as a teacher. Very often this ideal turns out to consist of a string of desirable character traits — kindness, honesty, generosity, integrity, loyalty, consistency, and so on. But an alternative, which I prefer, describes people not in terms of traits they possess, but in terms of how they operate — *process* rather than *contents*. One approach to what he calls 'self-actualizing man' has been spelled out by Abraham Maslow. Such a person is very much his own man — independent, resourceful and not bound by convention. He knows himself well — what he likes and what he dislikes — and is prepared to trust his own impulses and feelings, even if they lead in unexpected directions. He is never deliberately unconventional, but goes whichever way 'feels right'. Some people may find him a bit of a loner, but he is capable of great warmth, directness and spontaneity. Like a young child he enjoys finding things out, and has confidence in his ability to do so. He doesn't mind making mistakes or being seen not to know. He is capable of great absorption and delight in little things which may seem trivial to other people. He may well have more time for the people and events he comes in direct contact with, than for abstract discussions about great issues — for this reason he may appear to be rather socially irresponsible.

I find that SAM (self-actualizing man) is pretty close to my ideal of what I would like to be, and of what, as a teacher, I would like to try and help people become. But he's obviously not everybody's cup of tea. How does he strike you? The next question is relevant to the issue of whether schools ought to be producing SAMs or not.

Well-being is the state of having arrived at the full development of reason: not reason in the sense of a merely intellectual judgment, but in that of grasping truth by 'letting things be' (to use Heidegger's term) as they are. Well-being is only possible to the degree to which one has overcome one's narcissism; to the degree to which one is open, responsible, sensitive, awake, empty. Well-being means to be fully related to man and nature affectively, to overcome separateness and alienation to arrive at the experience of oneness with all that exists — and yet to experience *myself* at the same time as the separate entity *I* am, as the individual. Well-being means to be fully born, to become what one potentially is; it means to have the full capacity for joy and for sadness or, to put it still differently, to awake from the half-slumber the average man lives in, and to be fully awake. If it is all that it means also to be creative; that is to react and to respond to myself, to others, to everything that exists — to react and to respond as the real total man I am to the reality of everybody and everything as he or it is. In this act of true response lies the area of creativity, of seeing the world as it is *and* experiencing it as *my* world, the world created and transformed by my creative grasp of it, so that the world ceases to be a strange world 'over there', and becomes *my* world. Well-being means finally to drop one's Ego, to give up greed, to cease chasing after the preservation and the aggrandizement of the Ego, to be and to experience oneself in the act of being, not in having, preserving, coveting, using.

Erich Fromm

What is my responsibility to the children?

If you decide that some at least of your responsibility is directly to the children, rather than to institutions or societies, what exactly is it? Is it to help them become as self-sufficient, responsible for themselves, creative, critical, autonomous, individual, as possible? Or is it to help them to succeed in the world as it exists? These ideas aren't easy to reconcile. You may feel it right to encourage a child's own interest in motor-cycles, let's say, at the expense of his CSE's. But aren't you handicapping him in his ability to get a job? Do you have the right to stick to your ideology even though the children might suffer for it?

Do I want to change the System?

People vary in how their concern for children expresses itself. To take the extremes, A might be content to teach each of his classes as well as he can, and leave it at that, while B's ambition may be to become prime minister, or general secretary of the NUT, 'so that he can *really* get things done'. Everyone has to find his balance between doing a few children a lot of good now, and possibly doing a lot of children some good in the future. No one point on this scale is intrinsically any more worthy than any other; there's room for everybody. (One intermediate position is teacher training; there one trades first-hand contact with children for the chance of being able to reach more of them through the teachers. Another is *writing*, whether it be for the school magazine or the *TES*.) Don't let yourself be browbeaten by people who tell you that the *only* worthwhile thing to be is a Marxist/a member of rank and file/in educational research/etc.

What are 'children'?

Our current conception of childhood didn't exist in Britain in the seventeenth century, nor is it accepted in many parts of the world today. 'Extended childhood', which terminates either at 16 (leaving school) or 18 (gaining majority in law) according to choice, is a social institution, not a biological necessity. It may be that the kind of world we live in requires an extended childhood; there is certainly very much more to be learned about it than there was two hundred years ago; and if school prepares people for it, it may indeed be useful. But when one looks around inner London, say, one must at least question the wisdom of requiring physically mature 14-, 15- or 16-year-olds to spend half their waking lives, for three-quarters of the year, in a place many of them don't find relevant, and don't want to be in. Maybe the best way to learn about life is by living it.

In his recent book *Escape from Childhood*, John Holt compares our institution of childhood — which schools do an awful lot to support and perpetuate — to a walled garden. The theory is that this garden should be a place where young people can grow up sheltered from the majority of responsibilities and anxieties of the 'real' (adult) world. In practice, though, it can often feel not so much like a haven as like a prison, which prevents people who *want* to assume some or all of the rights and obligations of being grown-up from doing so. The question is: who holds the key to the door in the wall that leads to the outside — the teachers and parents, or the child himself.

What is my attitude towards children?

Do you *like* them? Do you feel comfortable with them? Are you ever aware of being condescending to them? How do your expectations of a 14-year-old differ from your expectations of someone your own age? Do you find yourself 'making allowances', 'knowing better', laughing (however kindly) at their slips of the tongue? If you do, and you reflect honestly, do you have any justification for these things? I heard or read of a woman in a shop who absent-mindedly gave a little boy she was passing an affectionate pat on the head. The 'little boy' turned and swore very loudly at her: he was a dwarf. Maybe *real* little boys feel insulted too.

Another discrimination we make is that we tend to 'like' or 'dislike' children *as a class*. All the questions at the beginning of this section take this sort of attitude. But children are individuals just as much as grown-ups are; why should we not accept that we get on with some and not others? I suspect that we tend to perpetuate the myth that everyone likes everyone else (even though children obviously learn the converse from their peers) largely because *we* are scared of being disliked (see next question).

Perhaps the fundamental issue is one of *trust*: to what extent do I have faith in children's ability to run their own lives, to take responsibility for their own actions, to select and seek out the things that they need? Do I trust them to turn out OK? Erich Fromm, in *The Art of Loving* argues that trust is a *sine qua non* of education:

> One of the most important conditions [for facilitating his growth] is that the significant person in a child's life has faith in his potentialities. The presence of this faith makes the difference between education and manipulation. Education is identical with helping the child realize his potentialities. The opposite of education is manipulation, which is based on the absence of faith in the growth of potentialities, and on the conviction that a child will be right only if the adults put into him what is desirable and suppress what seems to be undesirable.

This latter view is supported by C. B. Cox and Rhodes Boyson in the 1975 Black Paper: 'Children are not naturally good. They need firm, tactful discipline from parents and teachers with clear standards. Too much freedom for children breeds selfishness, vandalism and personal unhappiness.' Take your pick.

I think it's very important to be honest with oneself about this. It is fundamental to how one operates as a teacher, and to what one's ideals for education are. It is currently fashionable to pooh-pooh the Cox/Boyson attitude, in favour of an uncritical acceptance of a 'child-centred' view that is, to me, often naive in the extreme. Here again we are in an area where the 'belief–behaviour gap' is quite large: many people profess a Fromm attitude towards children, but act quite differently. 'Mummy wants you to do exactly what *you* want to do, Sarah. . . . Now you don't *really* want to do *that*, do you?' There is probably a lot to be said for giving children examples of adults who live clearly and honestly according to their own values, *whatever* they may be, rather than adults who seem to have no values at all. I have a lot of respect for people who act on their beliefs even though doing so may risk their friendships or their status. But it's hard enough to admit taking the Black Paper seriously — let alone agreeing with it — without being laughed at these days. As of November 1976 public opinion seems to be swinging back towards Cox and Boyson. But they remain dirty names in a lot of common-rooms.

If your instinctive reaction to the first 15-year-old you meet who can't write is one of alarm or horror, this issue is an important one for you.

Education should be gentle and stern, not cold and lax.

Joubert

What am I afraid of?

It is an exceptional person who doesn't have some fears about teaching. Although it isn't possible to make them melt away just by owning up to them, openly acknowledging them to yourself helps you not to be ashamed of them. Often the fear of the fear is much more debilitating than the fear itself. My fears include: fear of drying up (when giving a lecture), fear of looking stupid, anxiety that people won't like me, anxiety that they won't need me and a strong fear of physical violence. Other fears are fear of losing self-control, fear of sexual attraction (if you're a man in a girls' school, or vice versa, say), anxiety about invasion of privacy (the children finding things out about you), fear of noise and fear of uncertainty. I'm sure there are lots more: you can compile your own list.

The only way to tackle these things is to begin to find out that there really isn't anything to be afraid of. Many of them, it seems to me, are based on illusions that we could well do without – though of course they seem real enough at the time.

A man should not strive to eliminate his complexes but to get into accord with them: they are what legitimately directs his conduct in the world.

Sigmund Freud

What does 'equality' mean?

Good question! It's not at all clear. Here are some of the things it might mean. The question which underlies them is: which of them do you consider are important, worthy, feasible, or dangerous educational objectives.

1   Equality = identity
A lot of left-wing educational literature gives the impression

that it's jolly unfair that people should turn out to be differentially good at different things, and that it's the job of education to put this right. Let me just say two things about this. First, it is indisputable that people differ genetically (though any more precise claim is difficult to sustain), and in the extent to which their early lives fit them for subsequent activities, in particular, school. Second, the 'unfairness' of the situation only arises because society currently evaluates and rewards 'success' in terms of only one kind of ability, that is, the ability to do well at school (and for a few, at university). Success in school provides the passport for success, material and social, in the world at large. If worth was assessed not in one way but in lots of different ways, the 'equality requires identity' argument wouldn't be necessary. People would be allowed to be *different but equal*.

As an aside, we hear an awful lot about intelligence today, but precious little about wisdom. I don't know, but I suspect that, whereas intelligence is a measure of how good you are at one kind of thing, wisdom is a quality that derives from striving to be good at *anything* — it could be fishing or wood-carving as well as doing research or making speeches.

2 Equality of opportunity

Equality as identity means trying to rig the race so that the horses all finish together. Equality of opportunity means starting them together. And as Cox and Boyson say: 'You can have equality or equality of opportunity; you cannot have both.' Critics of comprehensive schooling claim its aim is to turn out people who are as-near-as-damn-it identical. Critics of public schools say that the race is decided before it's even begun. Is it possible to work out a better solution?

3 Equality of Esteem

In the day-to-day running of a classroom, these grand issues don't count for much. More important is the teacher's attitude to his pupils. It is vital, I think, to distinguish two ways they can be equal or unequal in his sight. The first I call equality of esteem: do you value all the children equally as people, not for what you might 'help' them to become, but for what they are? This quality has been described in a lot of different ways. Carl Rogers calls it

0379860

'prizing', or 'unconditional positive regard'. The 'unconditional' is important; it means 'I value *you*', not 'I will value you if . . .' or 'I would value you, but . . .'. John Holt describes A. S. Neill as having a quality of 'benign indifference', which I think is the same thing. It is an air of 'I love you, I care about you, but I don't *need* you. I don't need you to *be* anything and I don't need you to care about me.' If you don't have this attitude, you will only value people to the extent that they 'match up' in some way, to your system of values and expectations. Working with a classful of 15-year-old West Indians will be difficult under those circumstances!

A word of warning. Like everything else worthwhile, the establishing of this attitude (if you accept it as desirable) takes a long time. And it is impossible to fake it. When the chips are down, it may be better to be honest than to pretend. (I'm not too sure about this.)

4 Equality of attraction

It's absolutely essential not to confuse *valuing* someone with liking them. To value everyone of your students equally does *not* mean that you have to like them all equally. It's quite impossible to like any one person all the time, or to like everybody all at once. That's not the way we're built. To pretend otherwise is daft and dangerous.

When people start teaching, they often get upset because they find themselves attracted to a few 'favourite' pupils, and they think that this means they will be unfair. It may, but it needn't. Fairness is to do with how you administer your values, and the values of the school. Two things stand in the way of being fair. If you don't know your own values clearly, your judgments will be inconsistent and arbitrary. And if you need to be liked, you will be consistently unfair in favour of your favourites (because we need the people we like to like us more than we need the people we don't). The answer to the dilemma lies in cultivating benign indifference, rather than in denying the attraction. My bet is that children can appreciate the distinction between valuing and liking. A quote from Kohl again suggests they can, and also underlines the importance of acting from true conviction rather than out of fright.

Good teachers, according to the students, are generally the ones who are fair, do not lie, and are easy to talk

21

to. Strictness is not necessarily a defect. An honest but strict teacher is often considered difficult but worth having. A soft teacher is often made fun of. Students make subtle distinctions between teachers who are open because they believe in a free spirit in the classroom, on the one hand, and those who are 'easy' because they are afraid of the confrontation they may provoke if they assert authority.

Maybe another analogy that I didn't mention before is appropriate — good teacher as good parent.

Again let me stress this isn't easy. It takes time for people who like each other to be able to criticize each other. The bond of mutual 'valuing' must be firmly established first.

> Only strong natures can be really sweet ones: those that seem sweet are in general only weak, and may easily turn sour.
>
> *La Rochefoucauld*

Is there anything that I believe all children ought to be taught?

This follows on from thinking about the teacher–parent analogy. My 'ideal parent' contains a built-in paradox. On the one hand he has a value system that he believes in and tries to adhere to. He believes it is 'right', and wants to bring his children up to believe it too — whether it involves going to church, being kind to animals, fighting for your country, not telling lies or whatever. On the other hand, part of his belief-system is respect for individual freedom and responsibility, including his child's. And this requires him to allow the child to make up its own mind. The art of good parenthood (if a non-parent may make such a presumptuous claim) seems to me to lie in the struggle to resolve this dilemma.

Without any experience, I can't say how it's done. Obviously it depends on the age of the child. As he gets older, the balance presumably shifts from coercion and training to suggestion and discussion, thus developing his capacity to make choices, take decisions, and 'own' his own behaviour. The art is perhaps to do with the parent's being resistant to habit; it is very easy to slip into a fixed way of relating, and become blind to changes occurring in the other person. And it must also be affected by whether he (the parent) believes in his own values, and cares for his child enough to risk his anger: 'This hurts me more than it hurts you' is a grossly abused justification. It may also be, for the parent who cares, literally true (see next question).

To what extent these remarks apply to the secondary school teacher I'm not sure: I think at least the awareness of the paradox is useful. Jerome Bruner certainly agrees:

> Instruction is a provisional state that has as its object to make the learner . . . self-sufficient. Any regimen of correction carries the danger that the learner may become permanently dependent on the tutor's correction. The tutor must correct the learner in such a fashion that eventually makes it possible for the learner to take over the corrective function himself. Otherwise the result of instruction is to create a form of mastery that is contingent upon the perpetual presence of the teacher.

What are 'traditional' and 'progressive' teachers?

Absurd caricatures, that's what! And dangerous, too, because such oversimplifications are divisive and lead to polarized polemic, rather than any real communication. However, they can be useful fictional animals, and I'm going to run the risk of perpetuating the polarization by talking about them, because I want to suggest the possibility that what matters in dealing with children, as parent or teacher, is not so much what you do as the *way* you do it, and the spirit in which it is done. (This amplifies the remarks I made in the Introduction about how my beliefs have changed.)

The 'progressive' teacher sees his role, roughly, as being high on *support* and low on *directiveness*. His attitude is (again, roughly) 'I care about you enough to let you go your own way and do your own thing,' and what he means is that even though your goals and wishes may be different from his, nevertheless he has enough respect for and trust in your own individuality to help you achieve them. Yet it is equally possible to be 'pseudo-progressive', and say 'I care about you so *little* that I will let you do your own

thing' — which points not to self-effacing concern, but passive indifference.

Now let's look at Mr 'Traditional', who sees himself as being supportive too, but higher on directiveness. His sentiments are 'I care about you enough to make you do it my way,' by which he means that his belief in the rightness and morality of this course of action is so strong that it would be a disservice to his students, and immoral in his own eyes, to fail to pass it on — even though he may, at the time, reap only resentment and dislike. But, as before, it is equally possible for a 'pseudo-traditional' teacher to say 'I care about you so *little* that I will make you do it my way,' which is arrogant and authoritarian insensitivity.

The problem is that when the two sides confront one another, each tends to think the worst of the other — that they are hiding their basic indifference (which comes out as laziness in the 'progressives' and insensitivity in the 'traditionalists') behind waffle about liberty on the one hand and structure and discipline on the other.

What this line of thought suggests is that arguments about the relative merits of traditional and progressive teaching *methods* largely miss the point. If you look into your heart, know your own attitudes, sentiments, beliefs and priorities accurately and honestly, then the methods you use will, quite naturally, be right, authentic and effective.

Part 2

Some Practical Matters

Maxims are rules, the correct application of which is part of the art which they govern. . . . Maxims cannot be understood, still less applied by anyone not already possessing a good practical knowledge of the art. They derive their interest from our appreciation of the art, and cannot themselves either replace or establish that appreciation . . . maxims can function only within a framework of personal judgement.

M. Polanyi

This part contains a kind of dictionary of information, suggestions and thoughts. As before, the only person who can tell what will be useful to you is you. Many of the quotes from children are from *The School that I'd Like* — see Part 5.

Age

Teachers are often so far away from the age when they learned whatever it is they're teaching that they've probably forgotten the problems. Try and remember how difficult it was to grasp what 'differentiation' was all about, or what a 'noun clause complement' was. Children one or two years older may be able to explain it much better; do you have the opportunity to mix up the ages a bit, so they can learn from each other? If you've forgotten what it is like to be hopelessly baffled by something that looks as if it ought to make sense, but refuses to stand still long enough for you to grasp it, see how you get on with this sentence:

'We cannot prove the statement which is arrived at by substituting for the variable in the statement form "We cannot prove the statement which is arrived at by substituting for the variable in the statement form Y the name of the statement form in question" the name of the statement form in question.'

> Respect for the pupil is just as important as respect for the teacher, because after a young person's opinion has been disregarded three or four times the young person may never express an opinion again.
>
> *Sheila, 15*

> Everybody wants to *be* somebody; nobody wants to grow.
>
> *Goethe*

Anxiety

Most people seem to think anxiety is a bad thing. It isn't. It is simply the awareness that we do not have a ready-made response to meet the demands of the current situation. We will have to experiment with an answer or an action that will not necessarily turn out to be the best one. Now it is pretty obvious to me that such experimentation is an intrinsic part of being alive; if we could arrange our environment so that it didn't make demands on us, it would be incredibly tedious, and very different from the normal one. Therefore anxiety is an inevitable — indeed a useful — concomitant of learning. It is not something to flee from, or try to ignore. It is our organism telling our consciousness that there is learning to be done. A clear understanding of this can change your attitude to anxiety quite dramatically.

> People feel challenged when confronted with a problem that interests them and with which they believe they have a chance to succeed. People feel threatened when confronted with a problem they do not feel able to handle. Whether a child feels challenged or threatened is not a question of how it looks to his teacher — it is a question of how it looks to him.
>
> *A. W. Combs*

I have always thought it rather interesting to follow the involuntary movements of fear in clever people. Fools coarsely display their cowardice in all its nakedness, but the others are able to cover it with a veil so delicate, so daintily woven with small plausible lies, that there is some pleasure to be found in contemplating this ingenious work of the human intelligence.

De Tocqueville

Apologizing

You'll probably find yourself doing and saying things in class that you regret — and you'll have to decide whether to apologize or not, and whether to do it in front of the whole class. It depends on what kind of respect you want to maintain. If you feel as if an apology would be seized on as a sign of weakness, and reduce your authority, don't do it. But if you're trying to relate to the children as people, and act according to your principles (assuming you believe in apologies!), try it and see. You may find it increases, not decreases, their respect for you.

Apprentices

One old and out-of-fashion model of education is the master–apprentice relationship, in which 'A' sat and watched 'M', and slowly, by practising, absorbed his skills. You may find it helpful to attach yourself to an experienced teacher (during your teaching practice for example) who's willing to let you watch him at work. You may also be able to arrange for visits, or for people to come in to school, so that your children can watch people exercising *their* skills. During your first year or two of actual teaching, this may be useful, too. Schools differ, but on the whole teachers don't visit each other's classes and watch each other at work very much, which is a pity. But it may be worth a try — especially if you find you're having a hard time with a particular form, say, and you happen to know and get on with another teacher who manages to cope with them. You might just notice one or two significant ways in which his approach differs from yours if you sit at the back for a couple of lessons (provided of course that your presence doesn't lead the kids to put on a show for your benefit!).

Collusion

School teachers are often expected to stick up for each other. 'Staff can't be wrong' (cf. Apologizing). You have the choice, if you *are* asked to collude in this way, to (a) openly side with the child; (b) be studiously neutral and non-committal; (c) make an excuse and get out of it; (d) go along with the collusion, but take it up with the teacher later; (e) report the matter to the headmaster. (a) and (e) are difficult to do, and will certainly lose you sympathy in the staffroom and cause resentment. Only to be adopted when any other course would be a serious blow to self-respect (e.g. if you were disgusted with yourself for being 'chicken' on several previous occasions). Best done in cold, rather than hot, blood, so you're fully aware of what you're doing. If you adopt (d), which is more likely, remember people stop listening when they feel threatened. If your object is to make him think about the possibility he might be wrong, you'll have to tread softly. A row will only harden attitudes.

My fingernails are splitting because I think too much.
But please I cannot help it when I am so hungry.
Blackboard chalk tastes of memories on my tongue
— I built a wall and pulled it down.
But we are under heaven watching frogs
Spawning. Then Yoga next when we have tired
Of hen-or-egg infinity.
Pink-grey sun pricks needles in the scalp
Of my imagination. So fetch the paints
And this one sunset will not ever die.
And in my age shall I seek in the dusts of flesh
For some sad signs on which to weep,
As grain in a cockerel's craw.
Religions now: My Humanist views expounded forth,
Ground into dirt, to rise a swelling corn
To challenge god and prejudice.
The boy telepath down there is being trained
A different way from me. He knows no maths or history:
A moron, textbooks from the past would say.

But genius knows itself with calm.
And when the willow tree bends her back to laugh,
Then walk I, purple moon, with free breath.

Jeanne, 15

Competition

Liberal folklore has it that competition is bad — probably
because 'capitalism' is based on it. Training kids to be competitive may indeed be a necessary preliminary to the race
for the director's office. Maybe the schools could pay more
attention to collaboration, and suggesting the kids help
each other. But whatever your philosophy, it's a great big
competitive world out there; and children, in their games,
seem to be naturally competitive, and enjoy it. Your attitude to this may well depend on your politics.

Complaining

If you think you've been wronged, take it up with the headmaster (unless that's impossible) and if you get no satis-
faction, get in touch either with an HMI or the NUT.
Try and behave honourably, openly and coolly (e.g. inform
relevant people of what you're up to, be polite, etc.).

I attend a school set in delightfully natural grounds. I
do not fully appreciate this at my unperceptive age, but
cannot help feeling proud when its beauty is drawn to
my attention.

Sheila, 15

Confrontation (1)

Collusion is really a special case of confrontation: what do
you do when you run into a head-on conflict with another
member of staff? It might be useful to have thought before-
hand about under what circumstances, if any, you would
be prepared to risk your job. You probably won't be able
to come up with a list, but at least you'll have tried the idea
on to see what it feels like. The problem again is self-
respect: how much of a gap can you tolerate for how long

31

between the ideal and actual you? The more clearly formulated your ideals, and the more conscious of your own behaviour you are, the less 'avoidable' are questions of conscience like this — one good reason for not thinking too hard!

If you do decide you've got to do something, but can't face a row, write letters. It may be cowardly, but not nearly as cowardly as doing nothing. An advantage of letters is you can keep copies for future reference — sometimes quite useful. Also they are written in cold blood (usually), so you can be more composed.

Confrontation (2)

With the students, rather than with your colleagues, this time. The golden rule, which you will almost certainly have heard, is 'Don't have them'. This is remarkably little help — of course you will avoid them if you can, but you will often find you can't, especially in your first years of teaching, while you are gradually acquiring that subtle set of classroom skills called 'natural authority', and especially during your first few encounters with any new class. It is almost axiomatic that a new class will push you to find out what goes (particularly so if they are fourth- or fifth-year boys), and they will keep pushing until your 'No' is sufficiently loud, clear and unequivocal. But what *do* you do when you take your stand, tell Darren to sit down in your best no-nonsense voice, and Darren, drawing himself up to a full six inches taller than you, looks you in the eye and says 'Fuck off'? Well, you don't hit him, (a) because it's illegal, and (b) because you would get smashed to pulp if you did. You probably don't keep the confrontation going — all that will happen is that you get redder and unhappier while Darren seems to get bigger and bigger and cooler and cooler. It may well be time to call for help. If Darren is rioting, go and get hold of somebody — the first person that comes to hand who you think has the requisite level of 'natural authority' (or 'threat power'). If he isn't, back down temporarily but make it clear that 'the matter will be taken further'. Once things have got to this stage, you will lose face by calling in an outside authority — but you may lose a lot more by not doing anything.

Let me repeat that nobody in a sane situation would get

involved in some of the situations that you will get involved in, or resort to some of the tactics and ploys which you will find yourself resorting to. But you are there, voluntarily, in the classroom, eyeball to eyeball with Darren, and reflection on the lunacy of the whole business, or calling for institutional reform, will not get you through till break. And to find yourself doing unusual things in unusual situations doesn't mean you've 'changed', or 'sold out' or are a 'failure' — it just means that in unusual situations, you, like everybody else, will quite naturally behave in ways that surprise you. Nothing more. (See *Self*.)

Control

For many people, this is the magic ingredient. If you've got it, life's OK. If you haven't it's misery. Certainly it makes things a lot less fraught in your first term or so if you have the knack. To aim for 'control' is, as Paul Francis says in *Beyond Control*,

> a temporary device with a specific aim in view. It is limited, negative, unattractive and insensitive in that it fails to take account of individual differences. It treats classes as blocks, contained within subjects and sections of time in a quite unreal way, and it bears no relation to teachers' ideal image of themselves.

But if you want to be a teacher and the only way you can survive is in a 'hands-up', 'once-more-Timothy-and you're-here-till-five', 'now-I-want-you-all-to-copy-this-down' atmosphere, then that's the way it is. It's the problem of finding a style in which you can feel at home, and then working from there.

> . . . as imagination bodies forth
> The form of things unknown, the poet's pen
> Turns them to shapes, and gives to airy nothing
> A local habitation and a name.
> > *Shakespeare* (A Midsummer Night's Dream)

Let us learn to dream, gentlemen, then, perhaps, we shall find the truth . . . but let us beware of publishing our dreams before they have been put to the proof by the waking understanding.

Kekulé

Creativity

Creativity is often held up as being a worthwhile goal of education — to get people to think for themselves, to be able to produce and evaluate their own ideas, rather than just recording and parroting other people's. Yet both research and a mass of personal testimony show that the essential ingredient in being creative is to have time — to dream, to toy with ideas, to allow fantasies and images to come. And this kind of relaxed non-purposive atmosphere is conspicuously lacking in schools. Of course, one needs to absorb, think and read in preparation, and one needs to evaluate what comes afterwards, but unless there is an intermediate stage of 'incubation', what comes will be constrained by one's existing, conscious thought-processes.

It seems to me that if one looks for them, one may find many opportunities for allowing this sort of 'time out' for creatively playing with ideas — it can be done either individually or as a collaborative enterprise. It certainly needn't be confined just to 'creative writing'.

Curriculum

The big stumbling-block of a lot of fine ideals. With syllabuses to be covered and exams to be prepared for, there's not a lot of time left. If you are very radical you may ditch the syllabus entirely. Or you might allow ten minutes in every lesson for free discussion/time out/arbitration of conflicts, etc. Or you might allow 'red herrings' provided your syllabus is on schedule by the end of the week. Or you might not be able to tolerate any deviations at all. The best plan again is: find out what you feel comfortable doing, let the class know what the *rules* (q.v.) are, and move slowly from there as and when you feel the urge.

Discipline

A potential discipline problem arises when a child doesn't

do something that you've told him to do, or when you encounter a situation in which school rules are being broken.
There are three general things you can do: (a) Collude with
the children. If you can see no earthly reason why 14-year-
olds shouldn't smoke, you may 'ignore' it. The problem
here is that you might get a reputation among the children
for being easy, and get manoeuvred into conniving at things
you would rather not. Ask yourself whether you're acting
on the basis of a principle you're prepared to defend, or
are you 'sitting on the fence' and taking the easy way out.
(b) Deal with offenders in traditional manner (see *Punishment*). The children may not like it, but it's better to be
consistently authoritarian than a 'wishy-washy liberal'.
(c) Involve the children in the resolution of the situation.
Put the matter to the class, ask for their suggestions, and
accept them. Discipline at Summerhill was dealt with quite
successfully by the children themselves.

Often the words 'discipline' and 'control' are used inter-
changeably today. Many people prefer the latter, but I
prefer the former: it strikes me as both a more honest and
a more interesting word than 'control', which has for me
more sinister connotations of *Brave New World* and 'social
engineering'. Looked at from one point of view, discipline,
as L. L. Whyte describes it, 'ceases to be the attempted
denial of dissociated and distorted elements of the person,
and becomes education in the appropriate timing of
[action] .' There are times when it is most appropriate to
get out of the present situation what one can, to go for
'immediate gratification'. But there are other times when it
is best to forgo the instant pay-off in the interests of
achieving a longer-term objective. This view seems to make
some sense of the rather unfashionable notion of *self*-
discipline. Traditionally this has been associated with the
puritanical idea that it is inherently a 'good thing' to practise denying yourself things that give you pleasure. But you
can just as well see self-discipline as the (learned) ability
to weigh immediate and distant pay-offs against one another, so that you can act in ways which take account of
your *long-term* goals and well-being.

To have self-discipline in this sense is obviously a very
useful thing — it increases your options rather than decreases them. Young children are constrained by only being
able to see the immediate consequences, and it is no kindness to indulge them all the time so that they never get

35

beyond this stage. Thus it seems to me that there is a rationale for discipline which is genuinely benevolent; it need not always be (though of course it often is) callous and selfish. Whether you buy this rationale is, as always, up to you.

Educational psychologists

Sometime or other you may have a child in one of your classes whom you don't know how to deal with. The symptoms may be many, but one thing will be for sure: he isn't learning much. Your intuition will tell you either that he can learn, but he won't, or that he can't. In the first case he may be *maladjusted* or *emotionally disturbed* or *delinquent* or *psychopathic*. In the second he may be called *ESN (M)* (educationally sub-normal), *ESN (S)* (severely sub-normal, which is worse), *mentally handicapped*, *autistic* or *psychotic*. The first set of terms are variations on the ideas naughty, difficult and 'sick'. The second, stupid and mad.

After consultation with those pastorally concerned with him, and with the head teacher, an educational psychologist may be called in. His responsibility is to decide which label fits best by giving the child tests and talking to him, and either to try to sort him out himself or to refer him to a *Child Guidance Clinic*. He will come into contact with people with a bewildering variety of labels: school medical officers and health visitors, child psychiatrists, psychiatric social workers, education welfare officers and, if he's been very naughty, probation officers. In the main, their job is to make him better (if you're sympathetic) or to stop him being a problem and get him back to school (if you're cynical).

Part of the educational psychologist's responsibility is to 'communicate information from the Clinic that might be helpful to the teachers'; so he's the person to pester if you want to know how your child is making out.

Educational psychologists are in the main fantastically overworked, and have long working lists of children needing some attention. If your case worries you a lot, make a nuisance of yourself — things may happen quicker.

And don't let the fact that there are 'professionals' around put you off trying to help, yourself, if you want to and think you can. Despite the problems in 'befriending', a sympathetic grown-up whom a child knows (and trusts) may be more use to him than a horde of highly trained helpers.

Modern equipment? To me it's sheer poppycock. We want intelligent teachers and not machines. It is the poor doctor who hides behind a whole gamut of patent drugs.

Cosette, 17

Evaluation

This can mean different things. Most commonly it means 'you' imposing an assessment on 'them'. But it can also mean you and a child jointly discussing his work and deriving suggestions as to what to do next, or how to improve some aspect that you both agree needs improving. Thirdly, you can get the students to discuss and evaluate each other's work. You might be surprised how responsibly they do this if you try it.

When you try to be other than what you are, you give people expectations that are most unlikely to be fulfilled. To avoid being a serious disappointment to others you must accept and respect your own limitations. The difficulty of being humble, or even kind, is that it often requires that you be frankly selfish, that you discover your real feelings and follow them as if they were holy scriptures.

Alan Watts

Expectations

At the beginning of every year you'll probably get lots of 'helpful' information about your new class. Both 'good' and 'bad' pupils suffer because of this — they may feel so constrained by other people's expectations that they're not allowed to change even if they try. It is open to you not to read or listen to their potted histories, but to form your own impressions. You could even tell them that you haven't, so that they feel freer to change.

The students will also have expectations of you, which

you can meet or frustrate as you wish. They probably have a fairly fixed idea of what a teacher is supposed to be, and if you want to be something different, you must expect some resistance. Children are just as conservative as grown-ups.

Wise passiveness, followed in due course by wise hard work, is the condition of creativity. We do not fabricate our best ideas, they 'occur to us', they 'come into our heads'. Colloquial speech reminds us that, unless we give our subliminal mind a chance, we shall get nowhere. And it is by being wisely passive that we can most effectively help the subliminal mind to do its work. . . .

A habit of wise passiveness in relation to the everyday drama of the clouds and mist and sunshine can become a source, as Ruskin insists, of endless pleasure. But most of the products of our educational system prefer westerns and alcohol. . . .

Any method which promises to make life seem enjoyable, and the common-places of everyday experience more interesting should be welcomed as a major contribution to culture and morality. . . .

Watching and receiving in a state of perfect ease, or wise passiveness, is an art which can be cultivated and should be taught on every educational level from the most elementary to the most advanced.

Aldous Huxley

There is, it seems to us,
At best, only a limited value
In the knowledge derived from experience.
The knowledge imposes a pattern, and falsifies,
For the pattern is now in every moment
And every moment is a new and shocking
Valuation of all we have been. We are only undeceived
Of that which, deceiving, could no longer harm.

T. S. Eliot (East Coker)

New maths doesn't make any sense — just all measuring things that one will hardly ever have to measure in real life.

Isabel, 11

Experience

In 'traditional' education there was very little emphasis on direct experience. You didn't learn *with* or *through* things, you just learned about them. More recently, with the advent of discovery learning, Cuisenaire rods and Nuffield chemistry, people have acknowledged the value of experience in learning about various concepts the teacher has in mind. But the 'about' is still there — it's still learning 'about' — and I would like to see schools go one stage further and see the *intrinsic* value in experiencing. Everyone has had the experience of the simple but intense pleasure that results from becoming completely absorbed in the patterns in a fire, or in the smoke of a cigarette, the struggles of an ant with a crumb, the smell of hay, the sound of a rocky stream, the feel of another person's skin . . . 'the common-places of everyday experience'. As Huxley says, there are methods around (if you strip away the Oriental clothes, transcendental meditation is a reliable and effective one) which help to develop this capacity for absorption, for concentrated but effortless awareness of little things. But without sending your class on a full-blown TM training course (though this can and has been done) there are many opportunities open to you, whatever you teach, to allow children to explore the *textures* of the environment for their own sake without worrying, for the moment, about its *meaning*.

There is an old English saying: 'Sometimes I sits and thinks, but mostly I just sits'. Do not undervalue 'just sitting'. It is *not* a waste of time. Thinking isn't everything.

We live less and less and learn more and more. I have seen a man laughed at for examining a dead leaf attentively and with pleasure. No one would have laughed to hear a string of botanical terms muttered over it.

Gourmont

You teach your daughters the diameters of the planets and wonder when you have done that they do not delight in your company.

Dr Johnson

Friends

Should I become friends with the children? How involved can I get? These can be real problems. With the best intentions you may lead them to have expectations of you that are quite incompatible with the functions you are paid to carry out. When the crunch comes they may be very disappointed. Also, if your friendship leads to a confusion of liking and valuing (cf. Part 1) the other children may be legitimately resentful. My feeling is that the teacher–pupil relationship *is* a special one precisely in that there may be conflicting obligations. You are hired to *teach*, and any involvement that might conflict with that requires serious thought. If you are contemplating a sexual relationship, that requires *very* serious thought.

> I believe there is a definition of a teacher that goes something like this: 'A person who tries to impart knowledge to his pupils, even when they are listening to pop records, and, when he finds that he is not succeeding, sits and listens to them with his pupils.'
>
> *Barry, 16*

Fights

If a fight has to be stopped, you've got to be prepared to (a) sound very stern, and (b) physically restrain one of the protagonists, *or* have a sufficiently light touch to be able to talk them out of it in a jovial sort of way. If you can't manage that, pretend you haven't noticed, and hurry past. To have stopped it won't have solved the conflict that caused it. You may be able to help them sort it out peacefully.

(Soon after writing this, in October 1975, my flat-mate, who teaches in a comprehensive in North London, came home and told me about a fight at his school that day. About a hundred children were gathered after school in the road outside: the focus was a battle between two 13- or 14-year old West Indian girls, but some of the others were swopping punches in their excitement. A woman music teacher driving past decided she'd better stop and clear the road, but retreated to the staffroom after her glasses had been broken and her eye blackened. Six large male members of staff eventually dispersed the children. The music teacher wondered whether to prosecute. Fortunately, Eddie told me, they hadn't had a fight like that for six months.)

My few trite sentences look pretty sick in the face of stories of that sort. You really are on your own in situations like that and only your guts can tell you what to do. Nobody else can.

I myself would like more English and less arithmetic. English is so much more imaginative. The only imagination I use in arithmetic is when I guess the answers.

Melissa, 11

Flexibility

There will be situations when the rules let you down, especially if you try and meet situations as they come without forcing them to fit one of the institutionally approved moulds. It may not always be the 'class villain' who started the fight. If the children grow to trust you to be as fair as is possible, they may be very honest with you. On the other hand . . .

Honesty

Children can be very dishonest: reality tends to be what they want it to be. Very often you won't know whether you gave the detention to the right child. It may be tempting to shelve the problem by punishing everyone who could possibly have been guilty — or the whole class, even. (The ploy of deliberately punishing the whole group for a crime of one of its members is very successful at destroying group spirit — it was practised to good effect in German concentration camps — but it is not known to increase honesty.) In school it may create more resentment than it's worth.

Ordinary people are peculiar too:
Watch the vagrant in their eyes
Who sneaks away while they are talking with you
Into some black wood behind the skull.
Following un-, or other, realities,
Fishing for shadows in a pool.

But sometimes the vagrant comes the other way
Out of their eyes and into yours
Having mistaken you perhaps for yesterday
Or for tomorrow night, a wood in which
He may pick up among the pine-needles and burrs
The lost purse, the dropped stitch.

Vagrancy however is forbidden: ordinary men
Soon come back to normal, look you straight
In the eyes as if to say 'It will not happen again',
Put up a barrage of common sense to baulk
Intimacy but by mistake interpolate
Swear-words like roses in their talk.

Louis MacNeice

A French baby learns to talk first and then write: in
my school this is how it should be done.

Paul, 15

Ignorance

In order to assume the responsibility for your own learning,
you need two things — knowledge and confidence. Personal
creativity presupposes a firm understanding of the rules or
the structure within which 'self-appropriated' learning can
occur, for creativity without structure is anarchy, chaos.
In a specific sense we cannot create our own personal
theory about anything unless we know something about
it. And more generally we cannot direct our own learning
unless we possess the basic skills for undertaking the necessary exploration.

There are at least six such basic abilities without which
children will remain imprisoned within their own ignorance
and incompetence. The first is *concentration*, without
which one's learning is inefficient and fragmented. The
second is *sensitivity* or openness to the real nature of
things, without which one remains trapped by one's expectations and prejudices. The third is *sociability*, without
which one cannot enlist other people's help. The fourth,
fifth and sixth are basic *literacy*, *numeracy* and *rationality*,
without which one cannot read, calculate or think clearly.

To cling to a belief in 'individual freedom' to the extent
of failing to provide children with this rudimentary set of
core skills is, in my view, silly and irresponsible. Provided
your teaching of these things does not interfere with the
child's faith in his own ability to learn (and it needn't —
see *Skills* q.v.), I can't see any justification for not teaching
them.

The strongly motivated student who is faced with the
task of acquiring a new and complex skill may benefit
greatly from the discipline now associated with the old-
fashioned schoolmaster. . . . School has now made this
kind of drill teaching rare and disreputable, yet there
are many skills which a motivated student with normal
aptitude can master in a matter of a few months if
taught in this traditional way.

Ivan Illich

A teacher who was primarily concerned with being close
enough to the innermost meaning' [of his subject]
would be a very bad teacher. To be candid, I myself
have never said a word to my pupils about the 'meaning'
of music; if there is one, it does not need my explana-
tions. On the other hand I have always made a great
point of having my pupils count their eighths and six-
teenths nicely. Whatever you become, teacher, scholar
or musician, have respect for the 'meaning', but do not
imagine it can be taught. . . . If I were introducing pupils
to Homer, or Greek tragedy, say, I would not try to tell
them that the poetry is one of the manifestations of
the divine, but would endeavour to make the poetry
accessible to them by imparting a precise knowledge of
its linguistic and mystical strategies. The task of the
teacher and scholar is to study means, cultivate tradi-
tion, and preserve the purity of methods, not to deal in
incommunicable experiences. . . .

Herman Hesse (The Music Master, in *The Glass
Bead Game*

For all the talk in education about improving human
relations, fostering co-operation, and developing communication skills, very little has yet been done to en-
able pupils to react sensitively and constructively to the
feelings of other pupils.

Goodwin Watson

Intuition

People's attitudes to intuition vary. It is part of my belief system that intuitions are trustworthy, and valuable sources of information. You may have a hunch that Toby did it, or that Kevin really *does* want to go the toilet this time, or that the class is so fed up with Macbeth that you might as well stop. You can only find out if you're right by going along with it.

> A man should learn to detect and watch that gleam of light that flashes across his mind from within more than the luster of the firmament of bards and sages. Yet he dismisses without notice his thought, because it is his. In every work of genius we recognize our own rejected thoughts; they come back to use with a certain alienated majesty.
>
> *Emerson*

Jobs (applying for)

When you come to apply for a job you'll have a pretty good idea of what kind of school you would enjoy, or what kind would drive you insane in a week. If you hated your TP in an ILEA Comprehensive, there are lots of other schools around. You may be in your element with physically handicapped children, for example, while your room-mate, who sailed through her TP, wouldn't know where to start with them. Your training time isn't for proving yourself; it's for finding out, and *im*proving.

Find out as much about a school as possible. Don't accept it at its face value. A committed authoritarian head may be a better bet than a vacillating liberal one. Try and winkle out a member of staff whom you seem in tune with (it'll have to be a gamble) and ask him for his honest opinion. What kind of an atmosphere do the children have? Are they unnaturally quiet (or unnaturally friendly)? How do they react to the head teacher when they pass him in the corridor? Do members of staff have their own chairs in the staffroom (a dead giveaway for a stuffy school, I was told)? Decide before your interview how honest you are going to be: do you want the job at all costs, or do you only want it if people are ready to accept the real you?

I hear, and I forget;
I see, and I remember;
I do, and I understand.

A Chinese proverb

In learning there is no accumulation. Knowledge is different from learning. Knowledge is accumulation, conclusions, formulas, but learning is a constant movement without a centre, without a beginning or an end.

Krishnamurti

Learning

Learning is not something that people do or don't do, that they have to be cajoled into, interested in or rested from. Learning is something we are doing every minute of our lives — waking *and* sleeping — and which changes our process quite automatically in the light of experience. Imagine a stone rolling down a hill: as it rolls, it bumps into things (it 'has experiences'), as a result of which it gets smoother, and its rolling becomes easier. Most of our learning is exactly like this. This is what Krishnamurti means by learning.

What we teachers usually call 'learning' is what he calls knowledge: it is the accumulation of bits and pieces, nearly always expressed verbally, which do *not* change our 'structure'; they do not, on the whole, make our rolling through life any easier, they simply make our rolling through school easier. Accumulating knowledge is that special kind of learning that institutional education demands.

It is important to appreciate this, for it puts school learning and its relevance clearly in perspective.

They say that Rome has not died, she only sleeps — yet through all my pages of Latin verbs I have not felt her stir.

Gillian, 15

Medium

The medium is the message. The children will learn much more from what you are and the way you teach than from what you're talking about. In his introduction to *Mother*

Night, Kurt Vonnegut says: 'We are what we pretend to be, so we must be careful about what we pretend to be'. Be careful about what you pretend to be at school.

Messing about

In *Freedom and Beyond*, John Holt talks about the important stage in learning, before insight into the principles involved has occurred, of just messing about, familiarizing yourself with the words, symbols, tools — whatever it happens to be. Getting the feel of them. While I don't know any evidence about the benefits of messing about, it makes sense. Somehow or other you have to accumulate data in your brain *before* the principle that binds it all together can emerge. When children are apparently 'just' messing about, they may in fact be doing intuitively something that is important to smooth learning.

Schools don't explicitly allow time for messing about with learning. But you might be able to think of something — allow children to play games with the ideas, be silly for a while. (See also *Experience.*)

> The more a child uses his sense of consistency, of fitting things together and making sense, to find and correct his own mistakes, the more he will feel that his way of using his mind works, and the better he will get at it. He will feel more and more that he *can* figure out for himself, at least much of the time, which answers make sense and which do not. But if, as usually happens, we point out all his mistakes as soon as he makes them, and even worse, correct them for him, his self-checking and self-correcting skill will not develop, but will die out. . . . The result of this is a great loss.
>
> *John Holt*

> People who write textbooks do not make mistakes — and the best way to learn is by your own mistakes.
>
> *Jennifer, 15*

Mistakes

Like so many of these questions, whether and to what extent one should allow children to make, discover and correct their own mistakes is one that probably doesn't have a simple answer. On the one hand, I'm sure that John Holt is right; on the other it is sometimes dangerous, and often extremely wasteful of time, to refuse to point out and correct children's errors. This is a particular issue with backward readers, where if you don't point things out they will never get better, and if you point out every mistake they'll just get more and more fed up. My feeling, having faced this dilemma only last week, is that you have to rely on your intuition and sensitivity to the individual child's capacity and mood. What you need to develop as a teacher is not so much a rule of thumb, as this sensitivity.

Mistrust

Be prepared for any innovations you try to be greeted with suspicion. It will take a while for the children to accept that you are serious. Be prepared to be patient.

Motivation

There are two assumptions about human beings. One is that they don't do anything unless driven (motivated) to. The other is that we are intrinsically active, thinking, exploring, learning organisms. The first causes us to ask 'Why did he do X?'; the second 'why X *rather than* Y?' Most of psychology (and education) accepts the first. I prefer the second. It has the same sort of elegant feel to me as Newton's Second Law: it asks not why do things happen, but why do they *change*?

If you take the second view, it seems to me that motivational questions boil down to interest. 'Dan isn't motivated' means 'Dan has more important things on his mind than what you are offering him'. The key issue then is: does Dan need to be taught (now) things that don't interest him. Your answer to that is a personal matter. If Dan is young, you might be inclined to say 'Yes' — if whatever it is is important enough. But by secondary age there is more room for doubt, I think. (See *Learning*.)

> I would like to have teachers that are strict but not overstrict, who are feared by some and respected by all. . . . Nowadays that type of teacher is becoming obsolete, only to be replaced by over-dressed arrogant men who use long words to embarrass and trap people.
>
> *Barry, 16*

Names

It helps to learn your students' names as soon as you can: it gives them a feeling of being individually important to you. But beware, especially early on, of relying on names as an easy formula for instant intimacy. The children will spot it if you are trying to be too matey.

Get them to call you what feels right for you. If you don't mind them using your christian name, let them know, but don't force them. It may seem very unnatural to them.

Negotiation

You may find that as you gain confidence a lot of problems and decisions that you had assumed total responsibility for can actually be shared with a class. What to do with a persistent nuisance, how to organize the chairs, marking homework, taking the register, deciding what books to read, or where to go on an outing, where the tape-recorder has gone, how on earth to catch up on the syllabus . . . may all be things that are solved more easily, enjoyably and educationally in collaboration with the children, than on your own. Teachers who have tried it have been staggered at how co-operative, responsible and creative normally recalcitrant kids can be.

> . . . more outings during school time, field trips wherever it is possible to see the real thing, 3D education rather than flat black-and-white learning.
>
> *Anne, 18*

Nosiness

However good your intentions, children are as jealous of their privacy as you or I are. Don't think that caring is a licence to intrude. If you're genuine they'll come out to you as and when they feel safe to.

NUT

The National Union of Teachers is the biggest and most influential of the teacher's unions. In your first year it will cost only £5.00 (plus a smaller fee to the local association to which you belong), rising to £12.00 (plus local fee) after two years. For this you get general use of facilities, cheap insurance, and a free 'Countdown' discount card — and also the promise of individual advice and support if you need it. The NUT's legal department will help you if you fall out with school managers, governors, inspectors, local authorities, or the DES. The salary department will tell you whether you are being paid about the right amount, advise you on superannuation (pension rights), etc. The man to get in touch with is the regional official. If you work in Inner London he is Mr H. Perrin, Hamilton House, Mabledown Place, London, WC1.

Students can join the NUT as Associate Members absolutely free, and this gives you many of the benefits of a full member. You may use the legal service during your teaching practices, by contacting your NUT college rep., the secretary of your local NUT Association, or the Legal Department at Hamilton House directly.

Another bonus is NUT publications. Two that look as if they might be especially useful to students are *Treasure Chest for Teachers* (a mass of resources, ideas and addresses; price 90p) and *The First Teaching Practice* (price 50p). These are available by post from the Schoolmaster Publishing Company, Derbyshire House, Lower Street, Kettering, Northants.

Panic

This is the instantly recognizable feeling you get when things are getting out of control and you can't think of anything else to do. The veneer of liberal concern has cracked wide open and self-preservation is the only thing on your mind. Possible strategies are: go and get someone they're afraid of (effective in the short term, but entails loss of respect from kids, staff and self — it may be worth it, though) (cf. *Confrontation*); do something unexpected — see if you can stop them in their tracks for a moment and grab their attention. Try singing, settling down with a book, setting fire to the waste-paper-basket (a friend of mine has actually done this — it worked!), or running amok. When it's over see if you can talk honestly to them about what happened.

If you can accept that you will inevitably find yourself doing stupid, petty, vicious things at times, *without* losing sight of your principles, you will stand a better chance of hanging on to your sanity, and fending off the ulcer.

Parents

You will have to go to parents' evenings, and talk to them. As I keep saying, I reckon honesty is the best policy: if you can't remember who the couple sitting in front of you are talking about, you run less risk of blowing it if you ask them now rather than trying to bluff your way through. If parents want to see you as anything other than a fallible human being, that's their problem.

> I cannot go to my school,
> But must learn to live in your word-covered world,
> And learn about your things.
> Calling a leaf green instead of looking;
> And never knowing that in your lives you had
> Auschwitz. . . .
>> *David, 15*

Students often start their careers with some intense enthusiasm, and then learn in college how narrow and 'immature' it is, how much can be said on the other side, and how many other good ways of doing things exist. They gradually acquire a spirit of mellow tolerance and scholarly insight, but lose the creative impulse.

Weisskopf

Passion

There is not much passionate commitment to learning in schools and colleges: I suspect Weisskopf's description could apply to many, many people. Is there a happy medium to be found between fanatical and dogmatic belief, and dispassionate, dispirited, impersonal enquiry?

'Personal Relationships'

There are a number of courses appearing in schools, often masquerading as 'religious instruction' or 'community education' with names like this. There are things to be said both for and against them. The pros are obvious: they are new, interesting, trendy, lively, and at least superficially centred round the children's own worlds and interests. The main con that worries me is that they often seem to institutionalize the last private area of the children's school lives — their relationships with each other. How sad if this of all subjects were made boring by turning it into just another lesson. Also they are often seen by the students — quite justly — as bloody nosy.

Prejudice

Everyone has prejudices — in general they are predispositions to believe or expect or look for certain things in certain classes of people or institutions. But it's crucial to remember *these are only guidelines, not necessary truths*. The problems arise when we classify someone as a teacher, a Jew, black, Irish, an academic, a teeny-bopper, a priest, a mother . . . and treat them as *nothing but* the classification, or as X and *therefore necessarily* Y (Jewish and therefore mean, black and therefore violent, academic and therefore irrelevant).

Punishment

Detentions, lines, staying in during break, a visit to the head, and a beating are some of the weapons you have in your armoury of punishments. All of them are silly, and most of them seem totally devoid of deterrent-power. If you have to punish, and it is possible to make the punishment fit the crime, it is sensible to do so. But usually it isn't possible; school crimes aren't the right sort.

Corporal punishment is the most tricky. It can be divided into hot-blooded (a quick clip round the ear) and cold-blooded (a caning tomorrow). Both are ideologically unpopular at the moment; schools on the whole keep pretty quiet about it. But it may be, with the wisdom of hindsight, that we will be seen to be talking a load of cant about the psychological effects of hitting children. The hot-blooded sort, which provides an instantaneous expression and release of irritation, may be healthier in the long term than holding it in. I don't know. Anyway it's more likely to land you in trouble than a premeditated caning these days — children know their 'rights' quite well, and tend to get back at teachers by exploiting these rights.

You certainly aren't allowed to use corporal punishment while a student.

I admit that if all the teachers were oldish men it would be a bit rough on the physical education teacher, although a small fat middle-aged man as a P.E. instructor would suit me perfectly.

Katherine, 12

Relevance

'What's the point, Miss?' 'Why do we have to learn this?' 'It's boring' are familiar cries — and you may well be inclined to agree. If you do, you may be sure you won't be able to teach it convincingly, and it will be very hard to make it interesting. You might decide it's better to abandon the topic and have a discussion about why it's boring and what you can all do about it.

One central issue here is the relationship between what you are teaching and the children's home culture — they may be very different, as Spender's poem (below) makes plain. Should you concentrate on teaching things that are directly relevant to their immediate needs, or do you see your job as introducing them to wider, more general, sources of potential insight and delight? The former leaves you open to the charge of being condescending, under-

valuing the children's interests and abilities, and depriving
them, if they are 'working class', of the skills and knowledge
necessary to get on in, and manipulate, a world where the
'middle class' culture is the powerful one. The latter alternative runs the risk of trying to 'indoctrinate', or convert,
the children, to middle-class values, while implicitly or
explicitly devaluing their own attitudes and cultures. Again
this is an area where I can clearly see the values and the
risks in both attitudes, and where what one actually does
will probably be a complicated and intuitive synthesis,
deriving from one's own present and childhood values and
experiences.

> Far far from gusty waves these children's faces.
> Like rootless weeds, their hair torn round their pallor.
> The tall girl with her weighted-down head. The paper-
> seeming boy with rat's eyes. The stunted, unlucky heir
> Of twisted bones, reciting a father's gnarled disease,
> His lesson from his desk. At back of the dim class
> One unnoted, sweet and young. His eyes live in a dream
> Of squirrel's game, in tree room, other than this.

> On sour cream walls, donations. Shakespeare's head,
> Cloudless at dawn, civilized dome riding all cities,
> Belled, flowery, Tyrolese valley. Open-handed map
> Awarding the world its world. And yet, for these
> Children, these windows, not this world are world
> Where all their future's painted with a fog,
> A narrow street sealed in with a lead sky,
> Far far from rivers, capes, and stars of words.

> Surely, Shakespeare is wicked, the map a bad example
> With ships and sun and love tempting them to steal —
> For lives that slyly turn in their cramped holes
> From fog to endless night? On their slag heap, these
>   children
> Wear skins peeped through by bones and spectacles of
>   steel
> With mended glass, like bottle bits on stones.
> All of their time and space are foggy slum.
> So blot their maps with slums as big as doom.

> Unless, governor, teacher, inspector, visitor,
> This map becomes their window and these windows

That shut their lives like catacombs,
Break O break open till they break the town
And show the children to green fields, and all their world
Run azure on golden sands, to let their tongues
Run naked into books, the white and green leaves open
History theirs whose language is the sun.

Stephen Spender

History and geography are dealt with adequately, but
psychology and politics, drug-taking and smoking and
love and death are not mentioned in the school syllabus
at all.

Kari, 13

Remedial teaching

The organization of schools rests on the assumption that all
children who were born in the same year become ready,
willing and able to learn the same things in the same way at
the same time. If a child isn't ready, he is 'backward'. If he
isn't willing he is 'maladjusted'. Singling him out for remedial work may be sufficient, for one reason or another,
to help him catch up. On the other hand, it may reinforce
his feeling of being a failure and depress him sufficiently
for him to get still further behind. Much of the current
reading problem is due, I would guess, to the fact that we
insist on making a problem out of reading. (See *Skills*.)

Whether a child is sent for remedial help is a decision
that he ought to be allowed some say in. If he doesn't
want it to work, it won't.

Respect

There are two sorts: the sort you earn, and the sort that
comes with the job. You may need to fall back on the
latter, but I know which I'd rather have.

Rules

Don't believe any teacher who tells you that he doesn't
have any rules in his classroom. *Any* social situation has a

structure. There are things that go and things that don't. Situations differ in how many rules there are, and how explicit they are, not in whether there are any there or not. Often attempts to be liberal simply boil down to making the rules more difficult for the children to work out. Ideally the rules should be *few*, *explicit* and *sensible* (i.e. have some justification in the situation. Keeping quiet is often sensible. Being forbidden to chew gum seems much less so). With John Holt, I would say that what matters is whether the children know where they stand freedom-wise, and whether any offer of freedom is genuine, rather than how much is offered.

School-rules

Many of these will seem senseless to you; you'll have to make a policy decision as to whether you're going to enforce all or some of them or not, and stick to it. If you dither about, you'll end up confusing and upsetting everybody. Find out about the rules when you apply for the job. If you accept a job with your eyes open, it seems to me fair to expect you to abide by the rules that you know about. This doesn't, of course, stop you working to get them changed by persuading your colleagues, badgering staff meetings and the like.

Self

We all have an image about ourselves, about what kind of a person we are, and what we are capable of, based largely on how we have seen ourselves acting and reacting in the past. (It is also based partly on our absorption of *other people's* attitudes and expectations about us.) This image is based on what we *usually* do and feel in *usual* situations. The more constant our environment, the more closely we predict our own behaviour. But everybody, when they are faced by an *unusual* situation, reacts — *has* to react — in unusual ways. And this is in the nature of things, it is not something to get upset about. Our self-image is just a vague sketch of how we normally behave; it is not sacrosanct and we need not fret when we find ourselves doing something that appears inconsistent with it.

When we find a feature in the countryside that isn't marked on the map, we do not get agitated, or deny that the feature is 'real'; we know that it is the nature of maps to leave things out, and we can mark in the tower, or not, as we like. This is how our self-image is in relation to our real selves.

This is most important to understand, for, to begin with, school is an unusual situation, and it will elicit from you actions and feelings that surprise you. It is easy to get upset about this, and disclaim these actions as 'not the real me'. They are the real you, what is *not* is the self-image map which you are trying to defend. If you see your process of learning-to-be in school in this way, you need not worry about how you are turning out. Or rather, you can worry if your actions fail to meet the demands of the situation, but not if they fail to meet the demands of your self-image.

Self-consciousness

Learning to teach, like learning any skill that builds on existing habits, requires a stage of becoming aware of these habits and their effectiveness in the new context, breaking down, modifying and putting them back together so they work better, and then practising the new habits so they become intuitive and spontaneous once more. Of course things don't all happen in this nice neat sequence, but this is a general description of what one goes through. Self-awareness is a necessary and useful part of this process; it is not something to be worried about or fought.

However, self-awareness *can* become a handicap when it becomes chronic, analytic and evaluative, for then it consumes so much time and energy that it detracts from the action or reaction which was its original subject. This kind of negative, inhibiting awareness is what we call self-consciousness. A common example is when someone points out to you how much you say 'er . . . ' when you speak. Instantly your normal fluency (albeit er-spattered) breaks down — at least if you're anything like me — for two reasons, neither of which is actually necessary. First, you start *thinking* about it, wondering why you do it, wishing you didn't, etc., and all this activity competes with the actual business of talking. Second, you try not to do it, which also interferes, for it distances you from yourself, and creates an artificial distinction between the 'I' who doesn't want to say 'er', and the 'me', who does.

The answer is simply stated — though not so easy to do. Allow your awareness to tell you about yourself, without assuming that the you who is watching knows better than the you being watched.

Ghetto school teacher to Negro boy: 'How many legs does a grass-hopper have?'
Boy: 'Oh man, I sure wish I had your problems!'

Self-respect

This is a concept that keeps cropping up: it seems to be a critical one for the young teacher. It is a compound of (a) the size of the gap between what you would like to be, and what, given the constraints of your personality and of your situation, you can be, and (b) how big a gap you can tolerate. If the actual gap is smaller than the tolerable gap, you're OK. If it gets bigger, you're in trouble. In order to protect your view of yourself (see *Self*), you can either resign from the job, or have a nervous breakdown (which is a way of denying responsibility for your behaviour) or attempt to construe the school and/or the students in terms of stereotypes and prejudices that again prevent you from having to own your behaviour in the school. Many of the teachers one meets who have been working in difficult schools for a few years show signs of having adopted this latter alternative, though you may have to scratch a thinnish top-coat of liberalism before you see it.

Shouting

Shouting at a class is bad news. It may work once or twice as a shock-tactic, but if it becomes a habit you're on the run, and the students know it.

Silence

It is difficult to keep quiet if you have nothing to do.
Schopenhauer

Silence is the unbearable repartee.

G. K. Chesterton

These two little quotes say a lot about silence — or its absence — in the classroom, the first about how you get it, and the second about how you react to getting the kind you don't want (what teachers sometimes call 'dumb insolence').

Skills

Skills are useful knowledge; they are learnings which result not just in an expansion of what you can talk or write about, but in what you can do, in your competence. Learning a skill is rarely an end in itself — although the learning period may be enjoyable and/or hard work. What matters is the capacity to use the skill to read, write, drive a car, paint pictures, do research or teach. If the process of acquiring the skill (e.g. being taught it) undermines either your confidence to use it, or your enjoyment in using it, then that learning is self-defeating and pernicious.

School is full of examples of people who hate literature because somebody tried to teach them the skill of appreciating it, or football because they couldn't catch on as quickly as their mates. The many children who can't read are also victims of the vicious spiral in which initial failure saps confidence which causes more failure which saps more confidence. . . .

The point is that it is not *necessarily* damaging to be made to do, or learn, something — but it almost certainly is if you can't *do* it, as a result of inadequate intellectual or emotional preparation. 'As in our confidence, so is our capacity' says Hazlitt, and there is no more certain breeder of lack of confidence than failure.

Failure inhibits you in two ways. It inhibits your ability to use the skill you've got, and it inhibits your ability to get better. You underachieve, and you are *stuck underachieving*.

This has practical implications for you as a teacher. Provided the vicious spiral hasn't started, being directive and applying pressure may do no harm, and may well be helpful. Whatever your ideology, it's true that, on things they feel OK about, children like being stretched. But once the failure/lack of confidence spiral starts, your pressure can only exacerbate it. You have to change your tack, drop the pressure, and restore the child's confidence in his ability to learn. Even though you may not be able to implement this strategy-switch whenever it is necessary, it is important to be aware of its desirability, and sensitive to the presence of the spiral if it manifests itself in your pupils. At a rough guess, up to 80–90 per cent of a 4th-year class in a big inner-city comprehensive may be suffering from it.

It is also important to see that the spiral often manifests itself in widely different symptoms. The girl who never says anything and won't look up from her desk, and the boy who riots — when he isn't truanting — may both be suffering from it, and adopting different ways of coping.

> The common idea that success spoils people by making them vain, egotistic and self-complacent, is erroneous; on the contrary it makes them for the most part, humble, tolerant and kind. Failure makes people cruel and bitter.
>
> *W. Somerset Maugham*

Space

The way you organize the classroom physically probably says quite a lot about how you teach. Do all the desks have to be in rows facing the board, with your desk between them and it? Why not have the desks in small groups, or a circle, with you as a member of it? Is the blackboard your property, or can the children use it to work things out on? Can people see in through the door as they walk past? If so, do you feel like sticking a poster over the glass?

Many things in schools are taken for granted, simply because nobody bothers to think about them. If you develop a questioning attitude, to even 'trivial' little things, you will discover some interesting things that you might be able to do.

Spontaneity

Most of your training — this booklet included — can be seen as directed towards one end: undermining your spontaneity. Think about this. Is it good to do that? Do. Don't.

Do. Don't. You end up in the position of a mother who's read all the child-care books and is worse off than she was before, because she can't integrate all the different advice, and has lost her faith in her own intuition.

Despite the do's and don't's here, the main point I want to suggest is that the right thing to do is, on the whole, what *feels* right; and this is more a matter of intuition and spontaneous action than of reasoning. There are as many different ways of being a successful teacher as there are successful teachers, and more are being discovered, slowly, all the time. So no one can come up with a 'How to Become a Good Teacher in Three Easy Terms' formula.

But that's not to say that thinking is a waste of time. Somehow or other our thought-beliefs do manage to seep down from our heads into our bodies and become incorporated into the 'programs' that guide spontaneous action. The seepage won't be hurried, though.

Support

It can be pretty lonely in a school. If you can find another teacher there who thinks the same way as you do, and with whom you can be open and honest about your doubts, worries and mistakes, it will make a big difference. If not you might be able to meet weekly with some of your friends from your teacher training course.

Talking (to the children)

This isn't a bad idea, especially if you can make contact outside formal lessons — on a school trip for instance, or if you get involved with a club or society at lunch-time. If you want to, you could try devoting say ten minutes a lesson, or half a lesson a week, to chatting —about yourself and your interests to get the ball rolling, maybe. Like the English and German soldiers in the trenches in World War I exchanging presents on Christmas Day, if you can arrange little truces a bit of mutual understanding might develop!

It may be useful to question your motives (q.v.) for being nice and friendly to the children — talking to them, being concerned about them. You may be practising seduction. Are you *really* concerned, or does being seen to be concerned make them easier to teach? If they like you they won't play you up. And if they don't play you up you can persuade them to ingest French vocabulary quite painlessly. Is 'having the kids eating out of your hand' good for them, or only for you?

I think people are much more likely to remember facts if they enjoy having them told. A story helps, or plenty of adjectives.

Janet, 13

Teacher training

If you are still in training to be a teacher this section is addressed to you. You may be finding that some of the course seems 'irrelevant' or 'academic' to you, and that it fails to give you much good, solid, straight-from-the-shoulder practical advice about how to cope. The sad truth, I keep stressing, is that there isn't a lot of such advice to be given. What may be good and useful advice to one person may be worse than useless to another. This isn't just a let-out; it's true. Though of course what we *do* put into the course is open to criticism.

This problem often gets exacerbated because neither the lecturers nor the students are entirely explicit about what they can offer (on the one hand) and what they want (on the other). Lecturers are paid (presumably) to help students become good teachers, and cope with the stresses and anxieties on the way, so it's rather difficult to admit straight out that there's nothing much we can directly teach you that will ensure success. And you, unless you are pretty unusual, will be at least slightly nervous about how you are going to manage, and put the screws on us to provide the oft-mentioned 'survival kit' which we don't have. So there may be some frustrations and grumblings.

There is another, complementary, way of approaching your training. One of the most valuable things about teacher training is that you can feel what it's like to be taught. This probably wasn't important to you while you were doing your degree, but it is now. How do you feel when you're being lectured to? Do you prefer seminars? What sort of things bore you? Excite you? Make you angry? Try and get into the habit of standing back occasionally

61

and seeing how you react to things. Do you think children would react the same way? Do you care? You may find that the data you collect this way helps you to understand your students.

> To urge teachers to meet emotional needs without giving those teachers appropriate specialized training, brings [the danger] that they would again feel frustrated by one more educational 'ideal' which does not correspond to any practical skill they can be taught.
>
> *Goodwin Watson*

> A deadening influence in school is routine. Instead of obeying a set timetable, I would prefer to have my weekly quota of lessons supplied, and go to them in whichever order I liked according to mood.
>
> *Elizabeth, 16*

Timetable

The timetable and routines of school are to time what the classroom is to space. They are something that imposes organization. Just as you can give your students some say in the organization of space, so you can with time. If your subject is something they can learn for themselves, or if there are periods of 'doing examples', can you introduce a little flexibility about exactly when they do them? You could try and negotiate a bargain with them so that provided the work is done by a fixed time, you don't mind when. This sort of thing happens all the time in primary schools now; there's no good reason why it can't happen in secondary schools.

Trust

Do you trust the children to be fair with you if you're fair with them? Do you trust them not to steal things from the store-cupboard, or your purse? Do you trust them to own up? Do you trust them not to exploit your kindness? Two things are important in answering these questions: (a) do not prejudge this issue; let your trust develop from your own experience, and (b) don't be afraid to answer honestly 'No', or 'Only a little' to yourself. Don't confuse what you *do* feel with what you think you *ought* to feel.

Waste (of time)

You may find yourself reacting to a lot of things as 'a waste of time' — stop and ask yourself whether it is *really*. Senseless bits of school routine may give you the opportunity to talk to a few kids. Odd disputes and red herrings that crop up in the classroom may be turned to advantage. You might be able to drop your mask for a moment and cast some seeds of doubt about whether you really are the nervous, inconsistent, boring person that you spend most of your time in the classroom pretending to be.

Zen

The way to liberation in Zen Buddhism, as described by Alan Watts in *Psychotherapy East and West*, is to see through the artificial, conventional, illusory nature of social institutions. To realize that they are not 'reality', that things could be otherwise. School is a good place to practise.

> Don't get panarchy
> I don't want anarchy . . .
>
> *Paul, 17*

The day will inevitably come when what the educator thinks by word of mouth no longer works, but only what he is. Every educator . . . should constantly ask himself whether he is actually fulfilling his teachings in his own person and in his own life, to the best of his knowledge and with a clear conscience. Psychotherapy has taught us that in the final reckoning it is not knowledge or technical skill that has a curative effect, but the personality of the doctor. And it is the same with education: it presupposes self-education.

C. G. Jung

Part 3

Learning to be in School: A First-Hand Account

This part consists of an essay written by Anna Wilkinson after her second teaching practice, in May 1975, while she was taking the Post-Graduate Certificate in Education at the University of London Institute of Education. It captures for me many of the issues, problems, delights and frustrations which a new teacher almost inevitably has to face, in a vivid, lively, honest and amusing way. I am grateful to Anna for letting me use it.

I can't tell if you're serious or not,' said the driver.

'I won't know myself until I find out whether *life* is serious or not,' said Trout. 'It's *dangerous*, I know, and it can hurt a lot. That doesn't necessarily mean it's *serious*, too.'

Kurt Vonnegut, Jr

'Of course never turn your back on a class in school,' says my tutor wryly; 'and by the way', says my head of department with a smile when I first meet him, 'never leave your handbag anywhere.' I learn later that the French assistant lost ten pounds from hers the previous month. The deputy head smiles at me as well and says as she leaves me, 'Never go into the stockroom on your own with any of the boys, dear.' Tiny black clouds are gathering on the edge of my mind and I feel like Dante surveying the gates of Hell as he enters the Red City:

'Lasciate ogni speranza voi ch'entrate.'

I suppose that the Old Kent Road lashed by the rain and wind in November and pitted with bomb sites and half-eroded houses does look somewhat hellish seen for the first time. Under leaden skies I survey Lower School – huge and black and cracked on the outside, and on the inside echoing to its stone floors and white chipped tiles like some vast old Victorian loo.

I trudge out from the iron palings, black with age, and walk on through the rain to Upper School – by contrast a massive and modern conglomeration of concrete and glass blocks all identical to the unpractised eye and generally overheated. Under the streaking rain a few dark figures clad in a semblance of maroon and black lounge miserably against the concrete, shaking the drops from Afro hair and scowling.

Life was a series of continuous questions for at least a week: 'Where is G4?' 'Who is Roy Strand?' 'Where do I get the blue books from?' 'How do I mark a register?' 'What is the difference between . . . ?' The jargon soon becomes familiar. And endlessly, 'Where is . . . ?' Trying to find my way around the place and distinguish one twinkling set of glass panes from another was my biggest difficulty. A moment of panic and frustration as I spiral up endless concrete stairs only to end up in a science lab and not the staffroom. The library remained elusive for some time, as did the gym, and it was a very long time before I discovered that I was trudging three-quarters of the way round Block A to reach the staffroom when all that was needed was a short walk round the other side.

En route for the Big Hall (as opposed to multiple small ones) I stopped a scurrying member of staff one day:

'Excuse me, er, the Big Hall, could you tell me . . . ?'

Plump, startled, with the eyes of a nervous rabbit, her quick Scottish voice chipped in:

'Dunnae ask me where anything is, hen. I know my way from the staffroom to the Domestic Science Block (was that Block E or F?) and *that's it*,' and on she whirled resolutely, her eyes glued fixedly, and obviously, in the direction of the Domestic Science Block.

On the other hand, it did not seem to matter which pupil I stopped, big or small, they all could point out the way, they all could help, and it struck me that the size of the school probably worried the staff more than the kids, brought up as we were in small, sheltered secure little parochial grammar schools where silence was the norm and all was right in that corner of God's little world.

Most of the kids in this place charged around, loud and belligerent in their adolescence, voices raised ever higher, like small buffaloes trampling through rice fields. The girls gave sexy little giggles as they tottered around on massive platforms, adjusting their mascara and smoothing beautifully arched and plucked eyebrows. They were certainly very conscious of fashion, with their rings and bracelets and tight sweaters with plunging 'V' necklines, and would hold engrossing conversations with me between lessons about the length of my nails, or whether it was better to wear lipstick or lipgloss, and did I ever go to the disco at the Elephant and 'Are you married, Miss?'

'I want to get married just as soon as I leave school, Miss,' says Sally, 15 and leaving school at Easter. This meets the general consensus of approval. Heads nod, and Luisa, the Italian assistant, 29, unmarried and a blonde and liberated lady tries to offer alternative arguments in a commanding political voice. I join in, but so do other girls, all equally determined to be married as soon as possible.

'But why?' I finally ask.
'Get away from home, Miss.'

Suddenly I feel that I can't say any more, and that perhaps Luisa's and my arguments were not relevant after all. At least, I hope to myself, at least they can leave having had a different point of view put to them, and I am grateful that at least they talk openly about contraception, thanks to the breezy, unpatronizing seminars of the deputy head. A far cry from the coy little chats about rabbits at my own school.

It wasn't all good with the girls; sometimes I breathed deep in the heavy going of facing 13-year-olds who see me as some sort of competitive rival. I think of numerous lessons spent with third-year girls deaf to the world of French — and why not - smiling blissfully at pictures of Donny Osmond or the Bay City Rollers, or scribbling, very hard, on desks, 'Jenny and Steve, OK'.

'And why', I moan to my head of department, 'do the sixth-form boys have to play football right outside my window when the third and fourth years are doing French?'

Of course, unless they are at least 50, or an unprepossessing, mannish 30, and as ugly as sin, then women teachers are going to have a bigger struggle with some girls. I soon recognized that, especially with girls of 15 or so. Some could be very hurtful, the snide asides, the little grins, the sulks, the refusals, the blank stare, the little toss of the head.

'Wilkinson, you whore,' bellowed a female voice from the top of the science block as I was sauntering across to the staffroom. I grin to myself and pass on through the doors, glass held precariously in place by Sellotape, into the staffroom.

It is not only from the girls that women teachers have a problem, but inevitably, the idea is there that a woman is of necessity softer and kinder than a man. Well perhaps she is, perhaps not, but I found it annoying. Especially when team-teaching an unruly class of 15-year-olds one day with my very male head of department. Hand on hip he was verbally belabouring an argumentative Jamaican boy. Turning to me, hand over his head as if to wield off the force of his words, Denny looked cheekily up into my face and whimpered 'Miss, miss'. And being what I am I smiled, and it was only afterwards that the full force of what had occurred struck me.

Of course, I had to contend with a certain amount of being played off against another member of staff, as well, especially with this same form who were not too happy with the head of department. I often felt trapped into being more ruthless than I was, merely to hide the fact that I was being loyal to the staff. More than once I have hurriedly shot past a member of staff who is losing out in a slanging match because I secretly agreed with, well, not the member of staff.

'As you go out' called the head of department, standing by the main door, 'please hand your folders in to me.'

As if they were one, the entire class bolted out of the side door (where I happened to be standing) and Rose, who had publicly loathed me the term before, sweetly and neatly deposited the pile of folders into my surprised hands.

One thing I suffered from most of all in my first few weeks was utter exhaustion, and this despite the fact that as a student I was working little more than half a timetable. The sheer effort of being on your feet all day, of being constantly alert, never slacking and then going home to spend three hours or more preparing for the next day amazed me. No wonder the staffroom at a quarter to nine in the morning was full of red-eyed people, with tousled hair, draining coffee and pulling on cigarettes. By about half way through the first teaching practice I had physically adapted, but even so, there was the odd moment when I tiredly wondered whether 'jeudi' was spelt 'eu' or 'ue'.

During my free periods I would mark work, which I found very interesting, and I soon discovered I was what is known as an 'easy' marker, whatever that means. Otherwise, I studied the absentee lists in the odd quiet ten minutes. The big red bold 'absentee' notice was what had struck me when I walked into the staffroom for the very first time. The list from each form becomes progressively longer the higher up the school, and many names were a constant fixture, and many I hardly saw at all in lessons:

'Where's Suzy?'
'She's done a bunk, Miss.'

'Did you really go to football last lesson, Ian?'
'Oh Miss (exaggeratedly clutching his seventeen-year-old heart), would I lie to you?'

'Why does Roy have a guitar practice now when he should be in here with me?' (Innocent looks)

'But I *saw* Cathy at lunchtime buying an ice-cream.'
'It's me eye, Miss, got grit in it.'
'I think I ate something funny at lunchtime.'
'I've cut me finger (microscopic), can I go and get a plaster?'

'Miss, can I leave early to go swimming?'
'Have you got a note?'
'No, but I got all me kit.'
'Hard luck.'

As the weeks went by I found myself becoming progressively tougher. During my first practice I would probably have felt unsure and let Chris go on his mythical swimming trip, but, gaining ease and confidence in my second teaching spell, I was getting tougher decidedly, and I wasn't sure that I liked it.

'Well, how have you found teaching?' asked my tutor one day after the end.

'I never thought I could be so tough' I said slowly. He smiled as if to say that it was all part of the game, and I suppose he was right. But I still didn't think that it ought to be me versus them, or me not being me, but being tough and aggressive. The whole of the very first week of teaching had been spent in ridding myself of a horrible awareness of actually being — a teacher. That novel feeling was the worst thing; I didn't feel terribly sure either that I really ought to be telling other people what to do and how to speak, read and write French. I think that awareness probably saved me. I had decided not to act like the proverbial 'teacher', to forget the classroom, the desks, the uniforms, the mild shock of being 'in authority' and although I achieved this to a certain extent, insidiously, almost subconsciously, I was being forced to compromise.

'If you don't assert yourself with those first years now, they'll be an awful second year. You really ought to sit on them,' warned their form teacher. For whose good and for whose ultimate peace of mind? I often wondered. Granted, I did have a thumping headache by every breaktime during the first two weeks, but that wore off as I grew used to the general noise level of a school, and I smiled secretly at the puckered face of my tutor who had merely sat through a thirty-minute lesson.

'Have you got used to the noise level yet?' he would whisper as he wandered away. Nevertheless, I had to face it, part of me was wearing down, drop by drop, and I grew to tolerate less and less noise in the classroom. I refused to lose my temper, I refused to be other than calm, but I wanted less noise. I realized that, despite my disbelief when it had been suggested before by others who were wiser, my subject, French (or any language) needed a more con-trolled situation. Unfortunately, as in many other subjects, I could not encourage mass, continuous group-work for explorative purposes. Unfortunately, I was the only one in the classroom who could speak French to a reasonable degree of competence and so I *had* to have the attention and be listened to. I couldn't ask the kids to go off and 'discover' the perfect tense, like discovering that Mount Everest is on a map of the Himalayas. Therefore, I was faced with a bigger problem of assertion and dominance by the teacher than I had realized at first.

Noise never bothered me in the rest of the school — I enjoyed it and liked the atmosphere. It was a lively environment, natural, and not anathema to teenagers, nor was it silent and alien and sterile like a monastery. It never occurred to me to order people about and insist on absolute quiet and stillness in the school — as long as I had the strength to remain upright in the flood what did it matter?

The restlessness, the high spirits, the urge to fall off a chair, swing on a door, move around and poke the person next to you is a reassuring *need* for most of the kids, and I see this more and more.

But the conflict is still there, not just a conflict between the standards that I impose in the classroom, but the conflict in the fact that I *do* impose them and that part of my personality succumbs to this and part most definitely rejects it.

'You must be prepared to be more aggressive than your personality allows, and to come to terms with this if you feel it is worthwhile being a teacher,' says another tutor. Well, that is what I suppose I have done, and I am prepared to be criticized for doing so — I criticize myself — but the very fact that I am aware of what I am doing will, I hope, never disappear, and I will continue to work towards a situation where the conflict can be erased.

Gasping for a cigarette (why is it that the majority of teachers smoke?), I dash out at half-past three one afternoon through the rain and into the dark musty little sweetshop on the corner of the road, by Lower School. The shopkeeper smiles at me.

'Twenty Silk Cut please.' I smile back.

In the gloom, beneath my hand full of coins I notice two small 11-year-old figures, hands stuffed into black blazer pockets, hair damped to the forehead by rain. Trevor is plump and defiant, Charlie is abashed, clutching a bag of salt and vinegar crisps.

I look down coldly.

'Why aren't you in school?'
'We're goin' swimming'. Trevor is a dab offhander.
'Where?'
'Upper School.' Charlie has lovely big brown eyes.
'What time are you going?'
'Four o'clock.' Charlie doesn't stop to think.
'It is half-past three and it takes only five minutes to get there.'

Charlie shrinks back and two crisps flutter to the ground. I raise my eyebrows and Trevor still looks offhand.

'Who is taking you?'
'Mr Blakey.'

They shuffle in the silence and plod out of the shop wondering if they will have to face the head the next day.

'Mr Blakey,' I repeat as I leave.

Outside the rain falls on my face and I lean against a wet brick wall, over and over calling myself a cow. . . .
'You silly cow,' Wendy had called me only yesterday and I had only smiled, secure in the knowledge that I was not — but now I felt she was quite right, along with every-one else:

'Oh Miss, you do go on.'
'Who the hell do you think you are, bleedin' Raquel Welch?'
'Oh Miss, you do talk posh.'
'Don't she talk posh?'

I grit my teeth. It struck me that however good the rela-tionship was between you and a class there would always be a time when it was you who took the decisions, you who demanded things, imposed a way, refused a request, and when that happened you were you and they were thirty. The need, to meet the requirements of the school system, to be able to go in and teach a subject, to be more authori-tarian than my real personality, was one of the hardest things to accept on teaching practice, but there are times when I do accept it and act upon it without thinking.
Break never exists. I am sitting in the staffroom of the

Modern Language Block blissfully enjoying a cigarette and three smiling faces hammer on the window.

'Give us a drag, Miss.'
'Oh go on, just a drag, one drag.'
'Or even a blah.' (A 'blah', I learn, is a third of a drag!)
'Got a spare fag, Miss?'

I explain that just as they are not allowed into the Language Block at break, so I am not allowed to offer them a cigarette. This seems logical to some, but others merely pull bored faces.

A crowd swings on the bolted double doors to the block, glass smashes; the bolts, replaced three times already this term in progressively splintering wood, snap; screams, as a horde of 16-year-olds crash through the block and out of the other side. Desks overturn, tapes disappear, an overhead projector quivers and overturns . . . at the beginning of break people streaming from emptying classrooms take to stowing away in cupboards to be routed out by an endless and patiently searching staff. Cheers result for those crammed into ever smaller ones. I feel like offering them a currant cake with 'EAT ME' printed on the top.

'You're not aggressive enough,' said the director of the curriculum to me as he rose from watching me teach the last lesson of my second teaching practice. That gave me hope, especially as I was beginning to think I was never going to be rid of my layers of toughness!

'Be dramatic,' he said, with a grin. 'You've got to act it a bit.'

Act it? But I'd been struggling to be normal, and offer my own personality. And anyway, I really *was* interested in the responses, in the comments, and answers and people. I really did care how much a loaf of bread cost and what time they got up in the morning, and how many brothers and sisters, uncles and aunts they had (all in French, of course!).

'Try not to smile so much,' he continued. 'You tell them off and then you smile.'

'Can't you tell guilt when you see it?' I want to scream,

and besides, I could not envisage a lesson without a smile,
a laugh — I feel that to have a sense of humour and to show
it is the most important thing:

David and Mark trying to flatten down John's Afro
hair-do when they are measuring him in metres.

Peter in the first year putting on his jumper ('*Un tricot*'
shout the class),
and his tie — a little flourish — ('*une cravate*'),
and his blazer (the class yell, '*un veston*'),
and finally — another flourish — his coat (the class roars
in delight '*un manteau*').

An overheated classroom of overheated third years —
the height of the 'pass-it-on' episode, Kenny lolling
full length on a radiator fanning himself with the
curtains, chewing gum tossed around (I didn't feel like
catching it after it had been in Mark's mouth) — Johnny
Morris whining on the radio, patronizing us about
France (a new idea to grab the kids' interest) — a super-
latively useless exercise as I turned out to be the only
one in the room who wanted to listen, and that only
because I happened to have heard two-thirds of it the
night before and wanted, idly, to know how it ended.
Johnny Morris drones on. Outside a small group of
sixth-form boys lounged against a goal post, surrepti-
tiously smoking. Kenny softly opens a window, barks
out in his best and sternest impression of a teacher:
    'Hey you, boy, watcha think you're doin'?'
closes the window in a flash; the sixth-formers spin
round guiltily, startled — the third-formers scream with
laughter.
    'Hey Miss,' calls Leroy's deep Jamaican voice, as he
claps his hands, 'that sure deserved a laugh.'
    I had to admit he was right. And anyway it was at
times like these when I was enjoying my stay at the
school the most. It wasn't just a feeling of knowing
that the class was with you and that the teaching was a
two-way process, it was also a deep, relaxing feeling that
is experienced when a joke is shared.

Another of the nicest feelings in the world for me is when I
am with a group of people at the school and they are

evidently enjoying the French, and throwing out ideas of their own. I suspect that in a way I would have been happier teaching, say, History, as I soon discovered on teaching practice that French can be limiting because it is, above all, a cumulative subject, like Maths, and consequently has a degree of inflexibility which is unavoidable. However, that wasn't my biggest difficulty. It took a great deal to convince the kids that French existed outside the classroom, in fact, in France, and that living people used it as a means of communication just as they used English. Those who had been lucky enough to go with the school, or otherwise, to France came back ravished and delighted.

I ask a group of second years what they drank in France. The voices, enthusiastic, chip in thick and fast and they grin at me,

'du thé'
'de la limonade'
'du lait' (somebody kicks me under the table)
'du caf' (*'du café'*)
'du coca-cola' (giggles)
'Something a bit more alcoholic?'
'de la bière' (bien)
'du vin' (shouts)
Flushed faces and freckles survey me.
''Ere Miss what is a caf in French?'
'un café'
'But that's coffee. I mean a caf like 'ere where you get a cuppa tea. What's that in French?'
'It is "un café", just the same as coffee is "du café", that's where we get the name in English. You know, if you want a glass of wine in France you go into a café — "au café".'
'Wine — in a caf?' Others butt in:
'Course they drink it in a caf.'
'They drink it everywhere in France. All over the place.' (sniffs of disapproval)
''Ere Miss, why are French toilets just a hole in the ground?'

I find out that by and large it was the boys who created the laughs, who acted around and made the noise, caused the disturbance; but they were rarely as malicious as any girl who deliberately made trouble. The boys were so cool with their endless chewing, their quips and comebacks. At first I found the height and breadth of some of the oldest quite daunting as they cruised around with long, freaked-out hair, hands deep in fashionable baggy jeans; the regulation black blazer looked different on each boy and some wore with great style. They used to tilt forward on high-heeled boots, 'Wotcher, Miss,' and swagger on. That was Upper School, and the transition from Lower to Upper School wrought a bigger change on the boys than on the girls. At Lower School the boys seemed definitely very young, and some were so unbelievably tiny that you felt that the rounded cheeks would never sprout the hair that the 15-year-olds so cherished. I think of David in the first year with his pale round serious face covered in freckles — a moving fur-lined parka as he zooms into the room drowned in the garment, feet hardly visible, and his face and dark hair peer out of the depths. I think of Christopher, his face red and streaked with tears as he emerges from a second year's punch and of Desmond wandering round the Lower Hall with a black boa constrictor firmly wound round his wrist and a puckered frown on his forehead.

'Please, Miss, can you get it off?'

Together we carry the 12-foot reptile back to room G5 where it belongs to one of the music teachers, Michael, who sits oblivious to all, strumming on an old Spanish guitar and surrounded by a packed horde of eager jostling kids all poking, pulling and holding four other boa constrictors, a python, a rocksnake, three lizards (giant) and an iguana. By one o'clock almost half the school has squeezed into G5, and the door has to be locked. This happens at Lower School every lunchtime.

Upstairs in the staffroom at Lower School the atmosphere is cosy and very friendly, but as my practice wore on I noticed a slight rift between the two staffrooms of Upper and Lower School, and fewer and fewer members of Lower School attended the functions for *all* the staff held at the large Upper School staffroom. I felt this was a pity. Those members of staff who commuted between the schools, as I did, told me in varying degrees of privacy that they all preferred the 'intimate' atmosphere of Lower School. However, much as I liked and enjoyed the atmosphere at Lower School, I felt something was missing, and was infinitely happier in the open, rousing, less claustrophobic Upper School staffroom.

Lunchtimes were a laugh and I felt perfectly at ease in the staffroom. The staff were all very friendly, young and outgoing, and contrary to some of my friends' experiences, I never once heard any member of staff complain about their state as teachers in a futile and moaning way. They admitted the drawbacks and defects and sought to over-come them, and apart from the usual gossip, scandal and chat, I came to admire the atmosphere very much.

Lunchtime buzz invaded the staffroom, the unwrapping of sandwiches, buns, doughnuts, and a haze of cigarette smoke drifted and hung.

'Listen Jim, can you remind your form that they're in detention with me today?'
'Did you see Kenny's parents, Maggie?'
'Yes, most of that lot are going on the skiing trip at Easter.'
'Someone at the door to see Mr Bleathman.'
'Oh Christ, Linda, can you go down to the girls' chang-ing rooms, someone's throwing glasses out of the window . . . '

The first ten minutes was always about school and the day's immediate events, but, happily the talk was never solely about the school, or for that matter, anything re-motely to do with education. For that I was relieved, as I was also about their youth. Memories of my own school, stuffed with crabbed old Catholic spinsters like dried-up apples, had made my entrance into the staffroom here very apprehensive — I remember having a fleeting and ridiculous feeling of surprise at the amount of men, as, despite all, a traditional idea still held root at the back of my mind that teaching was something only women did. Second, it was the youth of the inhabitants of the staffroom which struck me forcibly, as it was to strike my boyfriend twelve weeks later at the staff party, despite the fact that I had told him.

Bedraggled from the rain and without an umbrella, I vaguely saw a black moustache, a pair of steel-rimmed glasses, a mass of blonde curls and long, jean-clad legs stretched out on top of little round tables. The moustache, I later discovered, belonged to Jim, who taught English with a struggle, as his long dark hair and long dark sideboards netted the girls who faced him dreamily behind the desks; and the blonde curls belonged to bubbly Jill who regularly lost her shoes in the staffroom; the glasses were David's, quiet and droll from the Maths department; and the jean-clad legs belonged to just about everyone save Simon, in his lemon-yellow shirt, fob watch and nice three-piece tweed suit. Simon elegantly pushing back flopping hair with a slim white hand, Simon who spoke nicely and quietly and langorously. . . . Why did the kids respond to him as in a spell and not make a move out of place? They adored him as they adored Chas, stocky and belligerent, who argued in Stalin's favour and made his classes howl in anger. And all that in Geography. And Jane with her straight black hair and intense, dark-shadowed eyes, who broke down in tears one day and all the third years solemnly apologized; and Mick, a quiet blonde dormouse; and Andy who swore at the kids as he chased them out of the library, and then swore again because they had made him swear.

'Got me paraplegic boots on today,' he said pointing to massive platform shoes.

The boys scoot out at that, but they are grinning. Segregation in Lower School is very strict and of their own choosing — all the girls sit together on one side of the room and all the boys on the other. This is especially strong in the first and often the second year too. I notice that in the second year boys who could be labelled as 'problems' are the ones who mix most freely with the girls — perhaps because they are less tolerated by their own sex, I do not know. However, it is generally considered a great hardship for a boy to come into a lesson late and be forced by lack of space to sit by a girl. Hoots of derision result, combined with little moans of horror from the girls, ever so proper. This attitude wears away and by the middle of the third year boys and girls mix freely and without much thought, save one day. . . .

'Please Miss, is that a boy?' Kevin's whisper is earnest and a little worried as he indicates Martin, aged 17, whose voice has not broken and never will. The nearest I ever came to tears was teaching Martin and his fellow fifth years, at least, I was not teaching anything and I was not being taught anything either, except how futile I could feel and how frustrated.

Screams of uncontrollable, ear-splitting laughter from Susan who was painting eye-lashes on Martin's pink cheeks (I didn't feel I could ask him to wash them off); shouts out of windows, exaggerated hair brushing, a transistor radio suddenly switched on and off, on and off; sodden chewed paper aimed with lethal accuracy at the head of Games who was supremely in control of an extraordinarily quiet football match three storeys below. A fight erupted between Marion and Sally — the third of the four fights I experienced — and I finally managed to persuade Sally to go and bathe her face. As she left the room and went outside she hurled a chair at the door for good measure. In all honesty I can say that I felt devoid of feeling. I didn't cry, I didn't shout, I didn't feel anything except how useless it all was. Wearily I switched off the overhead projector before it was unplugged from the back for the umpteenth time. Sitting on a desk facing them I suggested a discussion although I almost could not be bothered, but I did not feel that things were that hopeless.

> *'Jeudi dernier, au soir, une chose terrible s'est passée à Birmingham.'*

I was referring to the pub bombings and they were listening. We soon lapsed into English. They were responding ... the argument rose:

> 'IRA are bastards.'
> 'Course they oughta be hanged.'
> 'Hanging's too good for them.'
> 'Should be drawn and quartered slowly . . .'
> 'Hang 'em, I say.'

Looking at the heightened colour and hearing the edge of viciousness in the voices, I fought to remain, well, fairly neutral.

> 'Doesn't anyone believe in doing away with hanging?'
> I asked quietly.
> A calm and buxom girl looked up from her crocheting,
> 'I do, Miss.'
> 'Oh (relief) perhaps you could tell us why you feel like that, Karen?'

'I'm Irish.'

Nothing ever looked so black as that lesson, and I never again felt that momentary utter lack of interest in what I was doing and why. I felt that being calm had helped — I have only lost my temper once or twice and always regretted it, as I felt it was slightly ridiculous and completely ineffective. I think of poor Harry, the lumbering American, genial and gentle, who taught French alongside me. His lessons erupt regularly every five minutes with Harry bawling 'Quiet' with monotonous and irritating regularity. No doubt his class was quiet the first time he did it, but now it is something that happens every five minutes, just like the buses going by, and the response is nil.

Michael, highly strung and neurotic, ranted into a class of mine tearing his hair,

> 'I am trying to compose a flute descant,' he hissed into my ear, 'but that damn Yank interrupts every five seconds shrieking "quiet". Really, he couldn't control an out of work slot machine,' he spits, and flings himself dramatically outside again.

So the end of my second, and last, teaching practice sees me more confident as a person, more sure of my ideas and definitely harder in attitude — the latter, I suppose, was as inevitable as the toughening in my aggressive attitude. This time, by hardness, I refer to the hopeless feeling of not being able to help everyone, which I shall never lose, and the gradual adjustment I make to this situation. Looking at schools as they are, I have to accept the fact that if I concentrate on a few, desperate ones then the other twenty-five or so kids will lose out. I shall never forget the feeling of despair at my own inadequacy to remedy the situation, when I first saw and realized that there were children who could barely read three-letter words at the age of 12, 13, 14 and upwards. It sounds naive, but even as I had realized that this existed in our schools, I had to come face-to-face with it in reality, just as the kids had to go to France for French to become a reality to them.

In the first few weeks I could not stop thinking of this situation, but as time wore on I accepted it, or I think I would have gone mad. It will always, of course, be a prime part of my attitude to schools and education, but it will no longer dominate me as it did at first; thinking of Derek who could barely hold a pencil; Paul who spat at me in fear if I tried to help; Ozgul and Ayesha who could barely speak English, and Kim who sat morose behind her long, honey-coloured hair and etched thick biro marks right down both arms, and Peggy whose responses were unpredictable as a Czar's, 'I'm in a good mood today, Miss, sorry about yester-day'; Kenny chanting football songs through the lesson, and Katie, clutching at my skirt, wide-eyed, constantly be-wildered, trying to understand.

'Please Miss, are you the lady in the Cadbury's chocolate flake advert?'

Sometimes I think I must have been about as relevant as that to some of them. Someone they watched through unflickering eyes, who talked quickly, brightly and was gone.

It is crazy to talk about teachers taking the choice be-tween teaching and social work. It is a two-way process, and there is no choice. You may be teachers first, if you like, but unless you understand and are aware of the human problems and difficulties, and of the social environment of those you feel that you teach, then you cannot really be said to teach, or learn, anything.

Even if I didn't end up by 'coming out to see the stars' I felt I had learned a lot, enjoyed my teaching experience very much, and was very sad to leave the school. Turning round in the cold, half-past eight at night and the rain be-ginning to fall, I was just in time, as I silently said goodbye, to see David's fist go through a staffroom window as he stood silhouetted against the light, trying to warn some-body off the roof of the gym. Oh well, you can't win them all.

Part 4

Teachers and the Law

When I planned this book I imagined I could write a handy little reference section describing the legal rights, responsibilities and pitfalls in being a teacher; but having read about it a bit, I discover it's just not possible — the whole thing is too complicated. All I can do is pick out a few points that might be useful, and refer you to two excellent books, one by G. R. Barrell called *Teachers and the Law* (4th edition, Methuen, 1975), the other *The Parents' Schoolbook* by J. Stone and F. Taylor (Penguin, 1977), and to the NUT legal department. If you do get into problems or have doubts about things, expert help is really necessary.

Attendance

The children have to be there, and you have to do your bit to make them. It is legally necessary to keep an attendance register, accurately, in ink. If someone isn't there, you can mark him 'present' if he's at a medical or dental appointment, but under no other circumstances.

If a child fails to attend, his parents are guilty of an offence whether they know about it or not. Acceptable defences include (i) the child's illness, or (ii) if 'the parent has satisfied the LEA that he is receiving efficient, full-time education, suitable to his age, ability and aptitudes, otherwise than by attendance at school.' It is *not* an acceptable defence if the child is at home looking after a sick mother or sister.

Class-size

There is no statutory maximum number of pupils in a class.

Confidence

What children tell you in confidence clearly shouldn't be disclosed — except 'where there is a duty to do'. The circumstances in which this duty exists are not specified, but you have the legal obligation of any citizen to inform the police if the law is being broken — e.g. if you know your children are carrying cannabis. Whether you do actually shop them is your business, but you are technically committing an offence if you don't.

Confiscation

Permanent confiscation is theft, so be careful. If you confiscate anything valuable, it's best to give it back at the end of the day.

Disputes

(See *Collusion* and *Confrontation* in Part 2.) The school must inform you of who to get in touch with, how to do it, and what procedure will follow, if you have a dispute or grievance. In disagreements with a fellow teacher, any senior teacher (head of department, headmaster, etc.) has an obligation to help you try and sort it out informally. If this doesn't work, you submit a 'note of grievance' (explaining what it's all about) to the headmaster. He reports to the governors, and they arrange formal meetings to resolve it.

The NUT code of practice requires that any report about another teacher should be given to him to read, and that he should sign a statement saying he has done so.

If you are on the receiving end of suspension or dismissal, say, you have the right to attend, with a friend, any meeting of the governors or LEA where the matter is discussed. They must give you a clear seven days' notice of any such meeting.

Incidentally, the NUT code of practice declares it 'unprofessional' for 'any teacher to censure other teachers or criticize their work in the hearing of scholars'. So, if you refuse to collude, you will be violating the 'honour among thieves' solidarity of the NUT, and may incur its displeasure.

In loco parentis

The best and most general guideline about what is expected of you is this: 'The law requires that, since the teacher is *in loco parentis*, he should, quite naturally, take such care of his pupils as a prudent father would take. It does not demand more; it will not be satisfied with less.' (Barrell, op. cit.) In practice, I suspect this means not necessarily what you would do for your children, but what you imagine Mr Average would do for his; the man from Hendon, rather than from Hackney (at one extreme) or Hampstead (at the other). (These are horrible caricatures, of course.)

Negligence

To be negligent in law, you must (a) have had a duty towards X; (b) failed in it; and (c) X must have suffered as a result. The onus is on X to prove it. What this means is that genuine accidents — things that couldn't have reasonably been foreseen and guarded against — aren't your problem.

Your defence against a charge of negligence is stronger if (a) you have warned the children of possible danger, and (b) if what they were doing was against school rules. So if there's any doubt, give a warning.

'Failing in your duty' means falling short of what could have been expected of *a person like you*. You as a teacher are expected to be more knowledgeable about children, the kinds of things they get up to, and how to cope with them, than the man-in-the-street, so your responsibility is correspondingly higher.

It may seem unfair, but if you *voluntarily* accept responsibility (e.g. by seeing children home, helping them across the road, driving them to hospital in your car, or supervising a school outing) the law of negligence applies quite as firmly as for ordinary in-the-line-of-duty responsibilities.

Punishment

Again the main yardstick is the 'reasonably careful and caring father' one. All LEAs have some rules about punishment; it pays to know them.

Corporal punishment is obviously the most tricky. The law upholds 'moderate and reasonable' use of 'physical chastisement'. But the use of an unorthodox or forbidden method of punishment (which seems to include boxing a child's ears, or shaking him) is frowned on. You mustn't use corporal punishment while on probation anyway.

Every school must have a punishment book in which all cases of corporal punishment must be recorded in ink, and so that if any alterations are made, both old and new entries are clearly legible. The headmaster is responsible for this book's completeness and accuracy.

Probation

This period is to make sure that you can actually teach, but it is also to provide you with a 'run-in' to the real business. LEAs are asked to see that schools give probationers 'favourable working conditions', and the opportunity for getting help and advice from the head or another senior teacher. In practice, you will very likely find that everyone has off-loaded their worst classes and duties on to you; so you have a legal right to complain about this.

Records

A pupil's history of attainments, aptitudes, interests and disposition *may* be recorded, but it is not legally required.

Supervision

You are not obliged to carry out extra supervisory duties like meal-times, playtimes and games, but it is normally expected.

Part 5

Books

You will have, or have had, a surfeit of books to read during your training. I don't intend to mention any more academic ones here. However, it might be of interest to give you a list of the books that I and some of my students over the last few years found mean something to us personally, in terms of becoming a teacher. Again it's important to say that none of them is an infallible recipe for success. Carl Rogers' *On Becoming a Person* is the most important book I've read; other people have found it boring, trivial and repetitious. Yet one student last year told me I'd got to read *The Waves* by Virginia Woolf, and I had to give up after thirty pages, I found it so pretentious!

The comments in quotes come from reviews, jacket blurbs, etc.

EDUCATION

Berg, L.   *Risinghill: Death of a Comprehensive* (Penguin, 1968).
A book about Michael Duane, who managed, against all the odds to get a *good* school going in Islington, only to have it closed by the powers-that-be. Full of hope (it *can* be done) and disappointment (how difficult it is to do it). Passionate, and undoubtedly partisan.
Look at Kids (Penguin, 1972).
Sensitive and insightful observations and comments on kids in action.

Bettelheim, B.   *Love is not Enough* (Allen & Unwin, 1952).
About the author's approach to teaching severely handicapped children. I find his heart's in the right place but his style irritates me a lot.

Hargreaves, D.   *Interpersonal Relations and Education* (Routledge & Kegan Paul, 1972).

It looks a bit academic and forbidding, but well worth the effort. Actually quite readable.

Holt, J.   *How Children Fail* (Penguin, 1969).
How Children Learn (Penguin, 1970).
The Underachieving School (Penguin, 1971).
Freedom and and Beyond (Penguin, 1973).
Escape from Childhood (Penguin, 1975
Instead of Education (Penguin, 1977).

All opinion-provoking and forming. *Freedom and Beyond* is my favourite: it's the most theoretical. Nicely written, and full of common sense — but I'm slightly suspicious of the plausible generalizations that slip through when your guard is down.

Kohl, H.   *The Open Classroom* (Methuen, 1970).

Kohl spells out his ideal classroom, based on a *real* mutual respect between teacher and students, and offers some practical steps to take towards it.

Thirty-Six Children (Penguin, 1971).

A moving and depressing account of a beginning teacher struggling to live up to his ideals in a crazy school atmosphere that seems hardly a caricature at all.

Reading, How to (Penguin, 1974).

(Excellent non-grammatical title!) 'No one need write any more books about reading.' (John Holt) — the only sensible approach to the subject I've read.

Kozol, J.   *Death at an Early Age* (Penguin, 1968).

An account of appalling hypocrisy, insensitivity and downright brutality in a contemporary school — predominantly black — on the East Coast of the USA.

Lyon, H.   *Learning to Feel — Feeling to Learn* (Columbus, Ohio, Merrill, 1971).

Lots of examples of humanistic education in action. Quite encouraging.

Neill, A. S.   *Summerhill* (Penguin, 1970).

A description by the perpetrator of one of the classic experiments in progressive education.

Rogers, C. R.   *Freedom to Learn* (Columbus, Ohio, Merrill, 1969).

'A view of what education might become.' My bible.

Voeks, V.   *On Becoming an Educated Person* (Philadelphia, Saunders, 1964).

I don't know if this is available in England. About coping with anxiety, frustration, rewards etc. of learning. '. . . helps students do, and do better, things they feel they should do.'

POLITICS

Buckman, P.   *Education without Schools* (Souvenir Press, 1973).
Some interesting essays by the English school of deschoolers.

Friere, P.   *Pedagogy of the Oppressed* (Penguin, 1970).
I find the sociologico-political jargon very hard to take but
if you're into it, fine. Describes the teaching and learning
of literacy as politically motivated activities.

Goodman, P.   *Compulsory Miseducation* (Penguin, 1971).
Bracketed together in my mind with Illich's *Deschooling
Society* and Reimer's *School is Dead* as the 'Penguin Primer
of Education'. Necessary reading but a bit heavy on ideology and polemic for my taste.

Illich, I.   *After Deschooling — What?* (Writers' and Readers' Publishing Co-operative, 1974).
Deschooling Society (Penguin, 1975).

Lister, I.   *Deschooling: A Reader* (Cambridge University Press, 1974).
A collection of post-Illich writings on deschooling.

Pateman, T.   *Countercourse* (Penguin, 1972).
Contains a critical article on Peters's philosophy of education and an excellent bibliography.

Postman, N. and   *Teaching as a Subversive Activity* (Penguin, 1971).
Weingartner, C.   The turned-on teacher's handbook of bright ideas, snappy
come-backs, practical suggestions and common sense.

Reimer, E.   *School is Dead* (Penguin, 1971).

PSYCHOLOGY

Bannister, D.   *Inquiring Man* (Penguin, 1971).
and Fransella, F.   An introduction to the psychology of George Kelly —
personal construct theory. Really makes sense in terms of
Watts's *Psychotherapy East and West*.

Blatz, W. E.   *Human Security: Some Reflections* (University of Toronto
Press, 1966).
'It forces you to think.' 'Each chapter, each sentence, each
word provokes questions which only the reader can answer,' etc.

Cantril, H. and   *Reflections on the Human Venture* (New York University
Bumstead, C. H.   Press, 1960).
'Uses literature to illustrate concepts in psychology.' 'A
book of quotations taken from the literature of the world,

and woven into one of the most comprehensive books on man that I have ever read.'

De Bono, E. *The Mechanism of Mind* (Penguin, 1971).

It's fashionable to pooh-pooh de Bono — but I think he says a lot of quite insightful things, in a clear and simple way, about learning, memory and thinking.

Teacher Thinking (Temple Smith, 1976).

An entertaining and useful book if you are actually interested in *doing* what the title says, rather than using it as a weak excuse for teaching Latin, or Maths, or any other 'subject'.

Fromm, E. *The Art of Loving* (Allen & Unwin, 1957).

Fromm gets as near as you can to an analysis of what love is, without making the exercise seem ludicrous. Love, for him, is a kind of creative resolution of the antagonistic pulls of *caring* for someone and *respecting* their status as an independent human being.

Hudson, L. *Contrary Imaginations* (Penguin, 1968).

A nice chatty discourse on creativity, and different styles of thinking.

Koestler, A. *The Ghost in the Machine* (Pan, 1970).

'A new model for human wholeness . . . has all Arthur Koestler's usual mastery of wit, clarity and readableness.' I don't entirely agree with the 'clarity and readableness', but this is a non-negligible book.

Maslow, A. H. *Towards a Psychology of Being* (Van Nostrand, 1968).

With Rogers, one of the fathers of humanistic psychology.

Rogers, C. R. *On Becoming a Person* (Constable, 1967).

A collection of essays describing Rogers's philosophy and its implications. The most important book I have ever read. Read it.

Encounter Groups (Penguin, 1973).

A more sober version of Schutz.

Rowan, J. *Ordinary Ecstasy* (Routledge & Kegan Paul, 1976).

An informal primer of 'humanistic' psychology — the psychology of whole people — and the applications of this view of man to, amongst other areas, education.

Schutz, W. *Joy* (Penguin, 1973).

The theory and practice of encounter groups.

Skinner, B. F. *Walden Two* (New York, Macmillan, 1948).

Between Freedom and Dignity (Penguin, 1973).

You'll love him or hate him, but you can't ignore him! I actually think he talks a lot more sense than people usually think.

PSYCHOTHERAPY

Axline, V.   *Dibs: In Search of Self* (Penguin, 1971).
'Deeply thrilling', 'literally could not put it down', etc. The gentle understanding of play-therapist 'Miss A' helps an intelligent but autistic 5-year-old to find himself.

Goffman, E.   *Asylums* (Penguin, 1970).
An easy-to-read set of essays on the appalling effects of mental hospitals *qua* institutions on their 'clients'. Equally applicable to school (for 'patient' and 'nurse' read 'pupil' and 'teacher').

Laing, R.   *The Divided Self* (Penguin, 1970).
The Politics of Experience (Penguin, 1970).
The arch-proponent of listening rather than doing as the basis of psychotherapy, of course.

Perls, F.,   *Gestalt Therapy* (Penguin, 1973).
Hefferline, R. This is a do-it-yourself gestalt therapy course, with some
and Goodman, theory as well. Lots of exercises to help you relate better
P.   to your body, your feelings, and other people. It's wasted if you just read it.

Smith, J. S.   *When I Say, No, I Feel Guilty* (Bantam, 1975).
'Are you letting people walk all over you? Are you being manipulated into sexual encounters? . . . The Bestseller on Assertiveness Training!!'

Szasz, T. A.   *The Myth of Mental Illness* (Paladin, 1972).
The Manufacture of Madness (Paladin, 1973).
Another anti-psychiatry writer, but I think he spoils his case with some bogus arguments. Worth reading, though.

Watts, A.   *Does it Matter?* (Pantheon, 1970).
This is it (Random House, 1972).
Psychotherapy East and West (Penguin, 1973).
In My Own Way (Jonathan Cape, 1973).
Nature, Man and Woman (Wildwood House, 1973).
The Book on the Taboo Against Knowing Who You Are (Sphere, 1973).
The Wisdom of Insecurity (Rider, 1974).
Extremely lucid accounts of the 'way to enlightenment' that made a great deal of sense to me. Readable, original and profound.

KIDS TALKING

Blishen, E. *The School that I'd like* (Penguin, 1969).
A collection of children's thoughts about different aspects of school, collected in an *Observer* competition a few years ago. Obviously they represent the views of literate middle-class children on the whole. You'll be surprised (maybe) at how conformist a lot of them are.

Mildiner, L. and *The Gates* (Centerprise, 1975).
House, B. An autobiographical 'novel' by two young truants in the East End, describing their reactions to school, and how they cope with them.

PHILOSOPHY

Capra, F. *The Tao of Physics* (Wildwood House, 1975).
This does two things — explains, in layman's language, the facts and theories of modern high-energy and astro-physics; and draws some striking parallels between the philosophy that is emerging, and Eastern mystical thought.

Flew, A. *Thinking About Thinking* (Fontana, 1975).
Subtitled 'Do I Sincerely Want to Be Right?' Flew draws on a wide range of work in philosophy and logic to show how fallacious much of our thinking is, and how we can improve it.

Frayn, N. *Constructions* (Wildwood House, 1974).
A collection of thought-provoking speculations, in little snippets à la Wittgenstein. Philosophy that *really* means something. You may be put off by the rather fruity style, though it didn't worry me.

Hudson, L. *The Cult of the Fact* (Jonathan Cape, 1972).
Both this and Polanyi are attacking the impersonal view of knowledge. Not only is education a personal process: knowledge is a personal (subjective) commodity.

Magee, B. *Popper* (Fontana, 1973).
A readable introduction to one of the philosophical 'good guys'.

Polanyi, M. *Personal Knowledge* (Routledge & Kegan Paul, 1973).
One of those books I've been meaning to read for ages: a reference that's always cropping up.

Toffler, A. *Future Shock* (Pan, 1973).
An important book about the effects of an accelerating rate of change in the world on people and culture.

Whyte, L. L.   *The Next Development in Man* (Cresset Press, 1944).
Difficult to fathom, but very interesting description, by a noted biologist in the 30s and 40s, of what he calls 'dissociated man' (that's you and me) and what he sees as the next development — 'integrated man'.

MAINLY FICTION

Bach, R.   *Jonathan Livingston Seagull* (Turnstone, 1974).
A simple, child-like story that illustrates Spinoza's 'the more you know of particular things, the more you know of God'. I enjoyed it, but some people find it a bit whimsical.

Barth, J.   *The End of the Road* (Penguin, 1967).
The Floating Opera (Doubleday, 1967).
Tremendously witty and perceptive first novels by the young (incredibly, 24) John Barth, and much better, to my mind, than his epics, *Giles Goatboy* and *The Sotweed Factor*.

Barthes, R.   *Mythologies* (Paladin, 1973).
Slightly ludicrous but fascinating sociological insights and speculations about contemporary myths, sparked off by things like wrestling matches and Omo.

Borges, J. L.   *Labyrinths* (Penguin, 1970).
Fiction (Calder, 1965).
A bit like Frayn. If you're into wild intellectual jokes and philosophical profundity/absurdity (e.g. Stoppard), you'll like this.

Brautigan, R.   *Trout Fishing in America*, and others (Pan, 1972).
Brown, P. C.   *Smallcreep's Day* (Pan, 1973).
A fantasy about working in a big factory. 'A most lucidly written nightmare and a pleasure to read for its prose alone. . . . Apocalyptic. But funny with it.' (*Sunday Times!*)

Castaneda, C.   *The Teachings of Don Juan: A Yacqui Way of Knowledge* (Penguin, 1970).
A Separate Reality: Further Conversations with Don Juan (Penguin, 1973).
The Journey to Ixtalan (Bodley Head, 1973).
Tales of Power (Hodder & Stoughton, 1975).
Young UCLA anthropology student becomes apprenticed to a Yacqui Indian 'man of knowledge', and sets out to discover a different 'reality'. The struggle to resolve the clashes between two incompatible conceptual systems is fascinating.

Green, H. *I Never Promised You a Rose Garden* (Pan, 1972).
An autobiographical account of a 5-year schizophrenic period in the life of a young woman. One of my 'ten most moving books' (along with 'Dibs') without a doubt. The therapist is the heroine again.

Hesse, H. *Siddhartha* (Pan, 1974).
Steppenwolf (Penguin, 1969).
The Glass Bead Game (Penguin, 1972).
Really excellent novels of self-discovery and the search for a life style and values that one can believe in. 'Hesse, eighteen years ago, wrote about what college students are searching for today.'

Huxley, A. *Island* (Penguin, 1970).
The antithesis to *Brave New World* — Huxley's Utopia, where everyone meditates, takes LSD, lives in extended families and is (it goes without saying) much happier than we are.

Kesey, K. *One Flew Over the Cuckoo's Nest* (Pan, 1973).
'A top-drawer reading selection because of the character of McMurphy, the continual machinations of Big Nurse, the potential for misuse of psychosurgery, electric shock therapy, and power itself, and the general tragi-comedy tone of the book' — but of course you'll have seen the film by now.

Laing, R. *Knots* (Penguin, 1972).
Very effective variations on the 'I know that you know that I know . . .' theme.

Lessing, D. *Briefing for a Descent into Hell* (Cape, 1971).
Tough reading, but worth it (I'm told!). The story of the descent into madness of a university lecturer 'periodically experiencing moments of profound doubt about the validity of his way of life and the values it rests on'.

Perls, F. *In and Out the Garbage Pail* (Bantam, 1972).
Autobiography of the slightly loony founder of Gestalt therapy. A mixture of conceit, bombast and sensitive insight!

Pirsig, R. M. *Zen and the Art of Motor-Cycle Maintenance* (Bodley Head, 1974).
An extraordinary collection of bits of philosophy, do-it-yourself mechanical repairs, and everything in between.

Vonnegut, K. Jr. *Slaughterhouse Five* (Panther, 1972).
The Sirens of Titan; (Hodder & Stoughton, 1970), and others.

You can, if you like, just enjoy Vonnegut. But there's a lot to be learned, too.

White, P.   *The Solid Mandala* (Penguin, 1969).
The Tree of Man (Penguin, 1970).
Excellent novels!

Woolf, V.   *The Waves* (Penguin, 1969).
An incredibly powerful novel — for those who can appreciate it!

Postscript

I hope to produce a better version of this some time, but in order to improve it I need as much feedback as possible about what bits you found particularly relevant/irrelevant/helpful/silly/thought-provoking, etc., and also what was missing that you would have liked. Please send any comments to me at 24 Woburn Square, London, WC1.